Christmas, 1994
To John, our favorite
captain!

Love,
Nancy, Sparky &
Ben & Hilary

ATLANTIC FOUR-MASTER:
THE STORY OF THE SCHOONER
Herbert L. Rawding

On a dark spring day in 1946 the HERBERT L. RAWDING dropped anchor in St. John's, Newfoundland, with her last cargo of Nova Scotia coal. It was a dark day for the RAWDING as well. Never again would those lofty topmasts sweep the sky above windswept water, nor her long jibboom point the way toward far horizons. The last active four-master would soon be shorn of her tall spars for the sake of diesel engines, which would shake open her seams and send her to the bottom within a year.

(Courtesy Freeman Wareham)

ATLANTIC FOUR-MASTER:
THE STORY OF THE SCHOONER

1919–1947

Captain Francis E. Bowker

MYSTIC SEAPORT MUSEUM
MYSTIC, CONNECTICUT
1986

This book is dedicated to those who owned and man-
ned the great schooners so vital to the prosperity and
growth of the United States and Canada, and to those
who have had the foresight to preserve the records
and photographs that document their existence.

Designed by Marie-Louise Scull
Composed by Mim-G Studios, Inc.
Type set in Trump Mediaeval
Printed by Nimrod Press,
Boston, Massachusetts.

First printing, 1986
Copyright © 1986 by Mystic Seaport Museum, Incorporated

Cataloging in Publication Data

Bowker, Francis E., 1917–
Atlantic four-master: the story of the schooner
Herbert L. Rawding, 1919–1947.
Mystic, Conn., Mystic Seaport Museum, Inc., 1986.
x, 96 p. illus. 20 cm.
1. Coastwise Navigation.   2. Merchant Ships   3. Schooners.
4. Seafaring Life.   I. Herbert L. Rawding.
VM311.F7.B6
ISBN 0-913372-41-2
ISBN 0-913372-42-0 pbk.

Manufactured in the United States of America

CONTENTS

Captain Herbert L. Rawding, the schooner's namesake, poses with his wife Anna and son Clare, ca. 1920. (Courtesy Mr. and Mrs. Frank K. Damrell)

FOREWORD

Few men alive today could write such a book as this and fewer still could do so with the skill characteristic of autobiography and sailing vessel history written by Captain Francis Bowker. As he writes, schooners become persons with their own virtues and faults and peculiarities, their masters characters to be admired or despised or pitied but always to be tolerated and obeyed.

Captain Bowker, "Biff" to his friends, spent his youth in several of the last survivors of a once huge fleet of large multi-masted wooden schooners. He loved the life and is able to convey his sentiments to his readers without imparting any false gloss to the rugged life it was. He was student of the life as well as of the vessels he knew, had a perceptive eye, a retentive memory, a well-kept diary, and an excellent command of the English language. Put these ingredients together and what results is a book of the sea, nonfiction to delight any reader who enjoys such literature.

Thanks to Biff's gift for descriptive writing, readers are enabled to experience vicariously just what he saw and felt. Witness his account of the *Rawding* running before a gale.

The wind increased still more that day. Several times we got too far off before the wind and the fore gaff jibed across with a tremendous CRASH! that shook the entire ship. We eventually lowered that foresail and the fore staysail. With only the jib we ran off under bare poles, before giant seas that raced after the vessel, towering over her stern as she sagged back into the trough from the last sea and then, with a mighty thrust, swept high in the air. The sea would roar by underneath and drop the struggling schooner into another great hollow, so that the next monster could race down with terrifying force to threaten and then sweep by in a furious rage at its inability to overwhelm the quarry. The wind moaned constantly in the rigging and occasional gusts would strike the vessel in a cloud of spray blown from the tops of the sea, laying the ship over from the force against her bare masts and shrieking through the taut wire stays.

This book is much more than a biography of the four-masted schooner *Herbert L. Rawding*, though it is that too. One learns about other vessels that were the author's training grounds, some of which he sailed in before the mast or as an officer, and some of which he merely observed as a knowledgeable visitor. One learns of the routine of sea life on a big schooner and how things were done in those far-off days of the 1930s when Biff and I were both young and sea-struck. He realized his dream of seafaring under sail and thus became the object of some envy on my part. But we've been good friends, sharing a common love for more than forty years, and my envy long ago turned to gratitude for his willingness and his ability to share his experience through the well-written pages of his several books. This is but the latest book, and there are many like myself who hope that it will not be the last.

CHARLES S. MORGAN
former Chairman
Maine Maritime Museum

Concord, Massachusetts
September 23, 1985

ACKNOWLEDGMENTS

This work has been accomplished in fits and starts over a period of some years, and some kind individuals who have lent assistance have not lived to see its publication. To those who will finally see the results, I hope the experience will be rewarding. To all who have lent a hand I wish to express my thanks and deep appreciation. In accomplishing this research, I have had the assistance of old friends and colleagues and have met new and generous strangers who I now count as friends.

I have drawn especially on the wisdom and research of such longtime friends as Charles S. Morgan of Concord, Massachusetts; Captain W.J. Lewis Parker, USCG Ret., who provided leads and photos; Andrew Nesdall of Waban, Massachusetts, who located the half model of the *Alcaeus Hooper* and the building photos of the *Herbert L. Rawding*; and Giles M.S. Tod of Hingham, Massachusetts, who offered leads and photos.

Mr. and Mrs. Frank K. Damrell, at the instigation of their son Robert, made a special trip to Nova Scotia to find information about Mrs. Damrell's cousin Herbert L. Rawding. This trip resulted in contact with Mr. Merrill D. Rawding of Liverpool,

Nova Scotia, and Mrs. Frank Rawding of Clementsport, Nova Scotia, both of whom provided photos and information about the family.

For information about the building of the ship I am indebted to Mr. and Mrs. Donald H. Roeske of Somerset, New Jersey; Mrs. George H. Hopkins of Stockton Springs, Maine; Mr. William H. Pendleton of the Penobscot Marine Museum at Searsport, Maine; and the *Belfast Republican Journal* of Belfast, Maine.

Special thanks go to Mr. Garrett I. Johnson, who may be deceased as I have been unable to trace him through old addresses or friends. Mr. Johnson was a frequent visitor at the Perth Amboy Drydock in the fall of 1941. After the war he provided me with over a hundred of his photos of the *Rawding*, and I have taken the liberty of using some in this work.

To Captain Winsor Torrey's daughter, Mrs. Ruth Johnston of Medford, Massachusetts, I am deeply indebted for the use of his journal detailing the *Rawding*'s 1940 voyage to Martinique and Aruba.

The Newfoundland Museum at St. John's led me to Mr. Freeman Wareham, the late Victor Butler, and Captain Alex Rodway, all of whom were extremely generous in providing information on the *Rawding*'s year in Newfoundland. Ms. Heather Wareham of the Memorial Museum of Newfoundland has also assisted.

The story of my first voyage in the *Rawding* was published in the now-defunct magazine *Ships and the Sea* in 1952. I have taken the liberty of using this material in somewhat altered and annotated form.

Both the Bureau Veritas and the National Archives in Washington, D.C., provided copies of valuable documents concerning the *Rawding*'s career.

So many other generous persons have given of their time and efforts that it is impossible to name them all. I would, however, like to make special mention of Maynard Bray, who took the lines off the half model used to model the *Rawding*; the Seaport's Publications Department—Gerald Morris, Andrew German, and Nancy Zercher—who have made production of this book such a pleasure; and Mim-G Studios—Mimmi and Lynn Scull—who have produced such a handsome design.

To my wife Carole go especial thanks for editing and typing my drafts, for encouragement, and for putting up with those things authors' wives put up with: papers and photos strewn about, curses at things that have been misplaced, and lack of attention to chores that should have been performed.

Crowell & Thurlow and the *Herbert L. Rawding* • *1*

It took over a century for steam and the internal combustion engine to drive commercial sailing vessels from the seas. At first, engines were undependable and apt to explode; they were also costly and took up a great deal of interior space, not only for the engines themselves, but also for coal to make the steam. However, as the years went by, the engines improved, steel hulls provided dryer stowage, and regularity of delivery could be insured. Even iron and steel-hulled square-rigged sailing ships were forced into the carriage of lower paying bulk freights.

In the United States and Canada, wooden ships could be constructed cheaply. The United States protected its ships from foreign competition in intercoastal trade. Until the building of the Panama Canal, this kept a number of square-riggers busy running manufactured goods to the Pacific Coast and Hawaii and returning with sugar, canned goods, and lumber. On the East Coast the fore-and-aft schooner was more practical to operate on the coastal routes, requiring less crew and less expenditure for masts, sails, and rigging. The large schooner was generally built with less draft and more beam than a square-rigger and could sail with a clean-swept hold; this eliminated the time and expense of loading and discharging ballast and, at the same time, allowed it to operate in fairly shoal waters.

From the end of the Civil War until about 1905, large schooners were built by the hundreds on the Atlantic Coast. Agriculture, industry, and construction swallowed cargoes of coal, lumber, and fertilizer hungrily and begged for more. Larger and larger those schooners grew, and more and more masts were added, until the seven-master, *Thomas W. Lawson*, proved too large for the New England coal trade. From about 1907 until the start of World War I, the construction of schooners fell off to virtually nothing, as steamships built specifically for the coal trade and tows of barges gave reliable delivery and proved cost efficient.[1]

Among New England's schooner owning firms was Crowell & Thurlow of Boston, Massachusetts, established in 1901. This concern was formed by Captain Peter H. Crowell, a retired shipmaster from West Dennis, Cape Cod, and Lewis K. Thurlow who had been a clerk in the shipping office of John S. Emery Company of Boston. In 1900, when the two men joined forces, they listed one barkentine,

Masts for the RAWDING aboard railroad cars, Stockton Springs, 1919. The masts for these big schooners were commonly Douglas fir, shipped by rail from the West Coast. These three ninety-eight-foot rough spars are still eight-sided, and must be shaped to size with broadax and plane. The RAWDING's foremast will be twenty-seven inches in diameter, the other three masts twenty-six inches. (Couresy Andrew J. Nesdall)

The windlass has just been installed under the forecastle deck. This was driven by steam from the donkey engine, as were the capstan and winches. The bilge pumps were also steam operated, which saved the crew much back-breaking labor. Another comfort enjoyed aboard these large schooners was the steam heat in the crew quarters and cabin, if the captain was not too penurious to waste coal for such a luxury. (Courtesy Andrew J. Nesdall)

four three-masted schooners, and two four-masters. From this modest beginning, the firm went on to become the largest operator of multi-masted schooners in the United States.[2] Although primarily concerned with the coastwise and West Indies trades, Crowell & Thurlow vessels travelled to all parts of the Atlantic.

The company did not invest in the huge five- and six-masted coal carriers. Their largest vessel was the *Jennie Flood Kreger* at 1838 gross tons, and the smallest was the three-master *John R. Fell*, at 281 net tons. Among the fleet was the *Bradford C. French*, the largest three-master built, at 968 gross tons. Between 1912 and 1921 the company also added nine steamships to their operations.

Shortly after the start of World War I, as U-boat warfare began to decimate the fleets of European nations, Crowell & Thurlow had reason to congratulate themselves. Freights rose to unheard-of heights and Crowell & Thurlow formed two subsidiary companies, the Atlantic Coast Company and Boston Maritime Corporation. Ship-yards were purchased in which to build vessels and some were built at other yards on contract. Vessels were also purchased from other concerns, and a vast fleet was established.

At yards in the Maine ports of Thomaston, Boothbay, Harrington, Rockland, Stockton Springs, and Camden, keels were laid and great hulls took shape. As managing owners and agent, Crowell & Thurlow held the whole complex operation to-gether. During the years 1916 to 1918, inclusive, 147 percent dividends were paid out to share-holders.[3] Riding the crest of a sea of prosperity, they launched ship after ship and sent them off with high, prepaid freights and war insurance.

By 1916 it was apparent that the war would go on for some time. The United States was still neutral, and American business hurried to cash in on the profits. Sailing vessels could be built quickly and cheaply; they did not require the huge engines, elaborate electrical circuits, and deck machinery, of steamships. A small donkey engine, either gasoline or steam, a windlass for the anchor, and winch heads for the halyards were about all that were required. A schooner keel could be laid in the fall and the completed vessel leave the ways by summer, with rigging in place and sails bent. Another factor in the economy of a large schooner was the fact that it could be operated by a smaller crew than either a square-rigger or steamship. A large, four-masted schooner required a crew of nine to eleven men; captain, mate, bosun, the donkeyman, cook, and four to six sailors. Steamships required about double the crew and much fuel. A square-rigger needed double the crew plus more sails and rigging than a schooner.

All along the coast, from Maine to Texas and from California to Washington, as well as on the Great Lakes, old shipyards were reactivated and new ones sprang up. There were still virgin forests where axes rang and tall trees tumbled, to be hauled away to screaming saws and on to the shipyard. Here, sawing and chopping continued as keels were laid, frames erected, and planking shaped. Adding to the noise, as the hull took shape, were the thump of mauls and ring of caulking mallets. The best built ships required about as much board footage of rough timber as they could later carry in a full cargo. Even under the pressure of shortages, there were some shipbuilders who did their best to maintain quality; others threw in any sort of material the inspectors could be persuaded to accept, and ''war built'' became a term that denoted skepticism as to quality.

Even after the Armistice, freights remained high, as Europe required vast quantities of material to rebuild and recover from the ravages of war. Completely unawed by the fact that the War Shipping Board was turning out hundreds of steam-

Looking the length of her deck, the RAWDING appears much longer than her 200-foot registered length. Despite the tool chest, no shipwrights are visible, so perhaps it is the noon hour at the Stockton Springs yard. The quarter bitts have been set in place and covered to protect them from the weather until they can be varnished. The covering boards and waterways have been installed, but the balustrade rail has not yet been put in place. (Courtesy Andrew J. Nesdall)

The shipyard mold loft and part of Stockton Springs are seen in this view from the forecastle deck of the RAWDING. Her headsails have been bent and rigged in preparation for launching.
(Courtesy Andrew J. Nesdall)

ships, Crowell & Thurlow still had vessels on the ways when the boom collapsed in 1921. Few schooners built after 1918 paid off their costs. Before long, five-year-old schooners that had cost $200,000 were being auctioned off for as little as $5,000. Caught in the debacle, Crowell & Thurlow's steamships were taken over by the Mystic Steamship Company, and their Atlantic Coast Company merged with the New England Maritime Company, with Crowell & Thurlow as managers.[4]

Herbert L. Rawding was a senior master in the Crowell & Thurlow fleet by the time a vessel was named for him. He had been captain of the company's three-masted schooner *Bradford C. French* when he applied for membership in the Boston Marine Society in 1904. At one time Herbert Rawding and four of his brothers all commanded Crowell & Thurlow vessels. They were described as "men who never indulged in the use of intox-

icating liquors or used tobacco . . . . They were men of tall stature, radiating energy and conviction of purpose; ingredients of successful men."[5] Remaining with the company, he had left the sea to become Crowell & Thurlow's representative at the shipyard that constructed his namesake schooner and several others for the firm.

In 1919 Herbert L. Rawding supervised construction of the four-masted schooner that would bear his name. She was built at the Stockton Yard at Stockton Springs, Maine, located on land owned by the Bangor and Aroostook Railroad. The Stockton Yard built six four-masted schooners between 1918 and 1921 under master builder James Parker.[6]

The *Belfast Republican Journal* covered the launching of the *Herbert L. Rawding* in its 2 October 1919 issue.

Last Thursday was a day of interest for all Stocktonites, since it witnessed the successful launching of the four-masted schooner *Herbert L. Rawding*, the fourth to take the water from the new yard. It was estimated that a thousand people were present. At 12:30 o'clock, the schooner left the ways and took a graceful dip, to the accompaniment of cheers from the crowd. She was christened with flowers and Poland Spring water by Mrs. W.H. Morrison, wife of one of the members of the Stockton Yard, Inc., assisted by her sister, Mrs. Fred Sanborn, who dropped the flowers as Mrs. Morrison broke the bottle over the bow and allowed the water to flow down the sides of the schooner, a

The **HERBERT L. RAWDING** on the ways ready for launching, 25 September 1919. With flags flying and launching party aboard, the RAWDING sits poised for her baptism and entry into the element that will become her home and eventual grave. (Bowker Collection)

fitting Maine "libation to the gods." Mr. and Mrs. W.H. Morrison, Mrs. R.E. Morrison, Mrs. Fred Sanborn, Mrs. L.E. Bancroft and Mr. and Mrs. C.N. Taylor of Wellesley, Mass., and guests Judge and Mrs. Mulligan of Natick, Mass., composed the christening party, and others, to the number of fifty, were launched aboard—a delightful sensation, as the vessel dipped in the water and rose like a bird. She is of graceful proportions and was "a thing of beauty," in her coat of white [sic] with flags and streamers flying. Her momentum carried her halfway over to Cape Jellison, and those on board returned in the shipyard launches. Captain Herbert L. Rawding, for whom the schooner was named, is a retired shipmaster connected with Crowell & Thurlow and has been inspector for the three schooners built here for his company. The schooner is 185 on the keel, 215 feet overall, 38.5 feet beam and 22 feet depth of hold, with a net tonnage of 1109, the largest craft ever launched in the harbor, she is equipped with all modern conveniences, having running water, a bathroom, steam heat and electric lights. The cabins are attractively finished in cypress and sycamore; the captain's room and cabin being finely finished and the galley is as model a little kitchen as any housewife would desire. The *Rawding* was entirely completed when launched and proceeded to Norfolk, under command of Capt. John McKown of Boothbay, where she will load coal for the Canary Islands and receive her permanent captain, Charles Glaesel of Boston.

With sails bent, rigging rove off, and stores aboard, she was ready for sea and did not tarry long to be admired. On 27 September, two days after her launching, the *Herbert L. Rawding* sailed from Stockton Springs for Norfolk, where she loaded a cargo of coal. She sailed from Norfolk under command of Captain Charles Glaesel on 14 October and arrived at the Canary Islands on 25 November. Proceeding on, she arrived at Buenos Aires on 22 January 1920, and sailed for New York on 3 February. Undoubtedly she loaded a cargo such as beef bone, hides, or linseed at Buenos Aires. She arrived at New York 22 April 1920. Next was a cargo of coal for Lisbon, Portugal, under Captain M.D. Sanders of New Bedford, and then a return to Boston with a cargo of salt. It would seem that she carried four well-paying cargoes in her first year. She had probably also gained her lifelong reputation for being big, slow, cranky, tender with a deckload, but strong.

Now began a routine of coastwise passages, mainly with coal and hard pine to New England ports. During 1921 the *New York Maritime Register* made note of her masters. In October she was under Captain Holden[7] from Jacksonville to Boston, Captain Higbee from Boston to Port Tampa in November, and Captain Skolfield took her from Port Tampa to Baltimore in December and January. This seems like quite a turnover in captains.

In 1921 the *Rawding* ventured into the Bay of Fundy and loaded a couple of cargoes of plaster rock (gypsum) for Norfolk. Though times had turned tough for sailing vessels, and most owners had laid up their schooners, sold them for a fraction of their cost, or found captains willing to burn them or run them on convenient rocks, Crowell & Thurlow kept their fleet busy and even bought a few more schooners.

Not until 1925 did the *Rawding* have a mishap worth reporting. In October 1924 she loaded lumber at Charleston, South Carolina, and discharged at San Juan, Puerto Rico. From San Juan she sailed to Turks Island and took a cargo of salt for Boston. On 28 January 1925 the *New York Maritime Register* reported: "Norfolk, Jan 24. Schr. Herbert L. Rawding, from Turks Island for Boston was reported in a sinking condition 100 miles east of Cape Henry. Cutter *Carrabassett* was dispatched from Norfolk to assist her. A strong N.W. gale prevailed at the time. The cutter later returned to Norfolk to refuel; was unable to find the schooner; Cutter going out again."

On 4 February, the *Maritime Register* again reported: "Herbert L. Rawding schooner before reported, passed in by the Virginia Capes Jan 31, in tow of C.G. Cutter Gresham. Arr. Norfolk Feb 2."

Whatever was wrong was quickly repaired, for she left Norfolk on 11 February and arrived in Boston the 22nd. Salt was a dangerous cargo for wooden vessels for it would sift down through the ceiling into the limbers and clog the pumps. Many a schooner foundered in this manner.

In 1926 the *Rawding* was again reported in the *Maritime Register*: "Miami Mch 28, Schooner Herbert L. Rawding from Key West with a cargo of cement grounded in channel yesterday but was later assisted afloat, no damage reported. Stmr Ester Weems in passing the grounded schooner grounded in the channel but later floated and proceeded."

The helmsman keeps the RAWDING running off under a single jib before a gale in 1926. The reel attached to the starboard mizzen shrouds was used for rolling the halyard up in violent weather to prevent its washing around the deck or trailing overboard. Such reels were not carried during the RAWDING's later career.
Photo by F. Slade Dale. (73.544)

The HERBERT L. RAWDING steps along with a fair wind on her quarter, 1926. On such a pleasant day, some of the crew have hung out their washing. The man on watch works on a blown out topsail. It is the kind of day when sailors are glad to be at sea.
Photo by F. Slade Dale. (73.547)

At New York in 1930, the HERBERT L. RAWDING unloads the last cargo of blackstrap molasses brought north by sailing vessel for the American Molasses Company. By 1930 even this bulk trade was dominated by steamships.
MONSANTO MAGAZINE, April 1946.
(Courtesy Charles S. Morgan)

September 1927 found the vessel leaving Eastport, Maine, sailing around Nova Scotia, and loading a cargo of lumber at Wallace, Nova Scotia, on Northumberland Strait, to be delivered at Portland, Maine. This voyage gives a foretaste of things to come. The *Rawding* did not carry a deckload well, and upon arrival at Portland the *Maritime Register* reported: "At Portland Oct 16 from Wallace, N.S. Lost part of deckload in heavy weather."

In the fall of 1927 the *Rawding* left Portland for Cabo Roja, Puerto Rico, loaded with molasses puncheons to be filled and brought back. She arrived back in Portland 14 January 1928, where she was hauled on the railway for normal cleaning and painting. She then proceeded to Norfolk and came to Boston, where, for the first time, she rested from her labors.[8]

At about this time Crowell & Thurlow went through another financial upheaval, and most of their remaining vessels were sold off at marshall's auction. The *Herbert L. Rawding* was sold to Lewis K. Thurlow for $1600.

Still working, despite the world economic collapse, the *Rawding* sailed from Boston for Mayaguez, Puerto Rico, with a full hold of empty barrels on 6 April 1930. She returned to Boston on 14 June, with molasses, but was sent on to New York to discharge.[9] After a couple of coastwise passages, she took coal out to Guadeloupe in November and came back to Wilmington, North Carolina. Records suggest that she then made a couple of coal trips to New England ports. The last mention in the *New York Maritime Register* is that she sailed from Norfolk to New England and passed Cape Henry on 25 July 1931. With the Great Depression worsening, she was laid up at the end of that voyage, along with a number of her sisters, at

Boothbay Harbor, Maine, and remained there until December 1936.

In the summer of 1934, a visit to South Street, New York, by the five-masted schooner *Edna Hoyt* set off a chain of events that led to renewed life for the *Herbert L. Rawding*. The *Edna Hoyt* was the last active five-master on the East Coast, and her arrival at South Street attracted thousands of visitors. Financier Dr. Herman Baruch, brother of Bernard Baruch, was a frequent visitor as the vessel loaded a general cargo of merchandise for Venezuela. These visits resulted in a lasting friendship between Baruch and Captain Robert W. Rickson, the *Edna Hoyt*'s master.

The *Edna Hoyt* was owned by the Superior Trading and Transportation Company of Boston, and under the management of Foss and Crabtree, her principal owners and managers, she was active and profitable. Foss and Crabtree had the rights to thousands of tons of goat manure produced annually in northern Venezuela, much of which was transported to the United States in their own schooners. A typical voyage for the *Edna Hoyt* was a cargo of coal to Martinique; then a sail downwind to Venezuela, where "goatina," as Captain Foss would call it, was loaded for Jacksonville, Florida, to be used as fertilizer. From Jacksonville a cargo of southern pine might be carried to Boston or Portland, Maine.

Captain Rickson was one of those capable Nova Scotian shipmasters who came to the United States and commanded many of the largest schooners in the coastwise and offshore trades after the 1890s. Although a very pleasant man to talk with, he was about as tough a "Bluenose" captain as ever trod a deck. In port he could relax in the cabin or ashore; at sea he was a hard man, but a fine seaman and shiphandler.

Captain Rickson and Dr. Baruch discussed the idea of purchasing one of the big schooners laid up

The HERBERT L. RAWDING at South Portland, Maine, after her rescue from the ships' graveyard at Boothbay Harbor, 1937. Her paintwork shows the ravages of sun, snow, rain and several years of idleness and inattention. The jibboom and jib club have been brought inboard, presumably for inspection.
(Courtesy Charles S. Morgan)

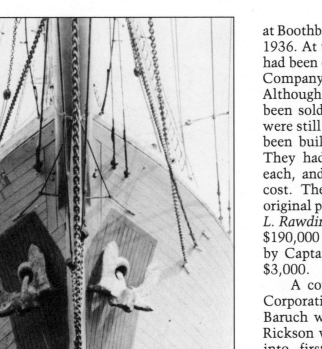

at Boothbay Harbor, but did not follow through until 1936. At that time, a number of big schooners that had been owned by the defunct Crowell & Thurlow Company lay idle and deteriorating at anchor. Although some of the best of the fleet had already been sold to Canadian and Finnish owners, there were still some fine vessels left, most of which had been built during and shortly after World War I. They had cost in the neighborhood of $200,000 each, and many of them never earned back their cost. They could be had for a fraction of their original price. Captain Rickson decided the *Herbert L. Rawding* was the best of the lot. Built at a cost of $190,000 seventeen years earlier, she was purchased by Captain Rickson for a reputed figure of about $3,000.

A company called the Kiraco Transportation Corporation was formed, of which Dr. Herman Baruch was actually the sole owner, but Captain Rickson was given *carte blanche* to put the vessel into first class condition. She was towed to Portland and completely overhauled. Although the hull was apparently in fine shape, she was completely recaulked. Her spanker mast showed some signs of rot, so was replaced by a good mast taken from another schooner. Both her standing and running rigging were replaced entirely, and a complete new set of sails came aboard. Captain Rickson assumed command, and on 9 June 1937 the *Herbert L. Rawding* sailed from Portland toward Newcastle, New Brunswick, to begin her new life.

Transformed from her dilapidated appearance of a few weeks earlier, the RAWDING lies at South Portland in 1937. Her bows look powerful and ready to face the sea in a new life. Beneath the battens that protect her planking from damage by her patent anchors can be seen the bowports that could be opened to load her hold with long timbers. Normally the ports were sealed and caulked tight. Sailors will note that there are twists in her outer and flying jib sheets, but Captain Edward Long, mate for Captain Rickson's passage to Newcastle, New Brunswick, would soon have everything shipshape. In the author's experience with Captains Long and Rickson, the crew of the RAWDING would have little time to sit around and wonder what to do with their hands. (Courtesy Charles S. Morgan)

Captain Rickson Commands the *Herbert L. Rawding* • 2

I first saw the *Rawding* when she was towed up the Miramichi River to dock at Newcastle, New Brunswick. I was a member of the crew of the four-master *Alvena*, which was docked about a mile upstream at South Nelson. We were quite proud of the fact that we had actually sailed up the winding river and saved the cost of a tow, but the size of the *Rawding*, her freshly scraped spars, new white paint on rails and houses and a fresh coat of gray paint, were a sight to remember. Any vessel Captain Rickson commanded was kept in yacht-like condition, and his crews never suffered boredom from lack of work.

As soon as our day's work was done, supper bolted down, and we were free to go, the crew of the *Alvena* trooped down to see this fine new arrival. Captain Rickson welcomed us in the gruff but pleasant manner he reserved for visitors, and we inspected the ship in a thorough manner. On this voyage the *Rawding* had four San Blas Indians in her forecastle, and I presume they were fine seamen. What a pleasure it was to see a vessel with all new sails, covered with white sail covers, and new shrouds with shining fresh tar on the serving. By contrast, the *Alvena* was an old schooner, run on a shoestring. If halyards parted they were not replaced, but rather spliced in the hope they could serve a while longer. We had blown out a couple of old sails coming around Cape Breton. The foresail wasn't considered worth repairing and, since the damage was below the reef, we just left it reefed, hoping the rest would last to New York.

Aboard the *Alvena* the loading of our cargo of lumber was delayed. The *Rawding* was to load a full cargo of lath; bundles soon filled her hold and began to be stowed on deck. One afternoon someone looked downstream and said, "What's going on with the *Rawding?*" All hands looked in some wonderment, for the *Rawding* was listed about ten degrees to port and there was no wind blowing off the dock. That evening we again trooped down to find what the problem might be. The *Rawding* was still listed over, and we found that Captain Rickson had refused to take any further deck cargo aboard. There wasn't much that could be done, once the cargo was aboard, and we saw them towed down the river with some apprehension, not quite so envious as when we saw that handsome vessel come in to join us.

(opposite)
Captain Robert W. Rickson was as tough as he looked. A bluenoser of the old school, he was born in Nova Scotia and came to the States as a young man, serving in a number of large vessels as master. Before taking the HERBERT L. RAWDING he commanded the five-masted schooner EDNA HOYT, the last vessel of her kind to sail the Atlantic.
(Courtesy Charles S. Morgan)

At the Bossert Lumber Company wharf on Newtown Creek, Long Island City, New York, the RAWDING discharges the cargo of laths it took her so long to carry from the Miramachi River to New York. The topmasts have been housed to clear the East River bridges, as she was towed to Newtown Creek from City Island. The main and mizzen gaffs have been rigged to hoist out the cargo. The towline has been coiled and hauled aloft to dry, presumably after being well sprayed with fresh water to remove the salt. When dry, it will be stowed below. Apparently the RAWDING had been painted while loading, and the crew, starting aft, had not been able to reach the waterline forward as the vessel had settled under her cargo. Already the polluted waters have turned her clean, white paint a dingy grey.
(Courtesy Captain W.J.L. Parker)

The J Boat RANGER slips by the HERBERT L. RAWDING off New London, Connecticut, in August 1937. The RAWDING probably awaits the turn of the tide and a little more breeze to continue her long, forty-six-day passage from New Brunswick to New York. At anchor, the RAWDING has only her main, mizzen, and spanker set to keep her head to the wind. The yawlboat is not on the davits, so perhaps Captain Rickson has gone ashore to report to customs or to telephone the agents to learn where he will be docking in New York. Since the RAWDING has been so long on her passage, a bit of fresh meat, fish, and vegetables may be in the boat upon his return. At the opposite extreme in sailing technology is the J Boat RANGER, the ultimate in fast racing boats of her day. While the RAWDING plodded along the coast that summer of 1937, the RANGER tore around the America's Cup course off Newport in a legendary performance.
Photo by Morris Rosenfeld. (83262)

Most American coasting schooners were built with flat bilges and enough beam-to-depth ratio to have a lot of initial stability. For that reason, coasting schooners seldom had need to take on ballast, an expensive and time consuming process. I don't know what thought went into the design of the *Herbert L. Rawding*, but on about the same length she was a bit deeper and had a couple of feet less beam than the *Helen Barnet Gring*, a similar schooner in which I later served. The *Gring* was steady as a rock with clean swept hold and could carry whole sail and topsails in a good, fresh breeze. Captain Rickson was discovering that his new ship was cranky, either light or with a deckload of lumber.

Captain Rickson soon had his fill of flopping around in this cranky schooner. As soon as the cargo of laths was discharged at Newtown Creek in Brooklyn, he loaded some sixty tons of rock ballast and had it permanently floored over. This meant sixty tons less cargo capacity, but a safer vessel that could stand up to a decent breeze.

In 1937 the Kiraco Transportation Corporation was dissolved. According to one source, when Dr. Baruch bought the *Herbert L. Rawding* he made just one stipulation: Captain Rickson could sail the vessel wherever he pleased and carry whatever cargo he could find, but the spare cabin must be available for Dr. Baruch's son at any time he might wish to make a voyage. One day Dr. Baruch asked Captain Rickson whether or not his son had ever made a trip. When Captain Rickson replied that he had never even seen his son, Dr. Baruch said in that case there was no use in keeping the vessel any longer and he would like to sell it to Captain Rickson.

Completely taken aback, Captain Rickson replied that he didn't have enough money to buy

From the deck of the four-master ALVENA off Pollock Rip, Cape Cod, the author photographed the HERBERT L. RAWDING in November 1937. Bound for Portsmouth, New Hampshire, to load scrap leather for Miami, she is "flying light" under three lowers and two headsails with a fresh nor'wester on her quarter.

the ship. Dr. Baruch inquired if he had a dollar. Rickson refused to buy the ship for a dollar, claiming that wouldn't be honest. Finally Baruch asked him to give the matter some thought and to let him know.

The next morning Captain Rickson came to shipchandler Edward L. Swan's office in New York to unburden himself. Mr. Swan listened to his story and then said, "Look, you old fool, if you don't take up that offer I'll buy her myself and you need never come back in this office again. Call Dr. Baruch this minute and thank him. If you don't have a dollar, I'll give you one!"[10]

It wasn't until 14 November 1937 that the *Rawding* again set sail, leaving City Island enroute to Portsmouth, New Hampshire, to load scrap leather for a fertilizer plant in Miami. Meanwhile we in the *Alvena* had made several passages and were enroute to Nova Scotia for another load of lumber. Although a fair wind blew, we anchored off Pollock Rip Lightship while the captain pondered whether to continue the voyage in a leaky vessel with worn-out gear, or put in to

Boston and again demand new sails and equipment. While we lay there, the *Herbert L. Rawding* came bobbing along, bound for Portsmouth. It was blowing fresh and the *Rawding*, high out of the water, boiled along under three lowers and three headsails and was soon out of sight. A while later, Captain Torrey made up his mind and we put in to Boston, where a couple of new sails and some rope came aboard.

On 27 November the *Rawding* left Portsmouth for Miami and arrived 16 December. From Miami she made her way to Mobile, Alabama, and loaded lumber for Santiago, Cuba. Sailing from Mobile on 21 January 1938, she again ran into rough going. On March 1 the *New York Maritime Register* reported: ''Santiago, Mch 1, Fears are entertained for the safety of the schooner Herbert L. Rawding which is overdue from Mobile with a cargo of lumber. The vessel was sighted off Santiago about Feb 18 but heavy seas drove her from the coast and she has not been sighted since.''

Despite the *Register*'s concern, on 7 March she was reported as having arrived at Santiago. From Santiago she sailed to Savannah and took lumber to San Juan, Puerto Rico. At this point, freights seem to have been hard to find, for she sailed back to Savannah, where she sat from 27 June to 2 November. She then proceeded to Jacksonville, where she lay from 6 November until 1 April of 1939, when she

The HERBERT L. RAWDING lies at Miami, where she has delivered a cargo of scrap leather to a fertilizer plant in December 1937. This photograph gives a clear view of the American shield painted on the end of the bowsprit. Such patriotic emblems were rather common decorations on American sailing vessels. Otherwise, the RAWDING has only a billethead and simple scroll decoration.
(Courtesy H.W. Stone)

left for Hampton Roads. It wasn't until 31 May that she sailed laden with coal for Bermuda and then to Haiti for a cargo of logwood to Baltimore, where she arrived on 27 August.

Again there was a layup before she was towed to Norfolk and loaded coal for Fort-de-France, Martinique, for which port she departed on Christmas Day. During this period, the *Rawding* could hardly be said to making anybody rich, but a war was brewing in Europe and freights began to look better.

In the fall of 1940, Captain Rickson sold at least part of the ship to Captain Harold G. Foss; Foss and Crabtree thus became managing owners. Captain Rickson retired from the sea and Captain Winsor Torrey took over as master.

Captain Winsor Torrey was one of the younger masters of large schooners. He was born at Deer Isle, Maine, in 1890, one of four brothers, all of whom became masters of large schooners.[11] When nothing better was offered, Captain Torrey sailed yachts in the Boston-Cape Cod area and in Florida. He did not like skippering yachts, but was not a man who enjoyed being idle. The *Rawding* was Torrey's last large schooner; as she was for most of us who sailed her in those years.

Miner G. "Bob" Robinson, the mate, was a different sort of man. Raised in Dorchester, Massachusetts, he often wandered the waterfront

The HERBERT L. RAWDING unloads her cargo of Haitian logwood at Young's Dye Works, Baltimore, 1939. The cargo she delivered on the author's voyage in 1942 proved to be the last logwood cargo brought north under sail. Photo by Norman G. Ruckert. (Courtesy Mariners' Museum of Newport News, Virginia)

as a boy. Bob was a graduate of Tabor Academy at Marion, Massachusetts, a school with a naval and yachting tradition. Bob certainly had salt in his blood. He and I were shipmates in several large schooners; our final voyage together was in the *Herbert L. Rawding*. During World War II, Bob joined the Navy and was lost at sea.

The *Rawding* carried coal to Martinique, proceeded to Turks Island and brought salt to Norfolk, arriving 8 March 1940. Shortly after arrival at Norfolk, the vessel was chartered and loaded a full cargo of coal for Trondheim, Norway. Going ashore to clear the ship, Captain Torrey was confronted with news that Germany had just invaded Norway. For a couple of months the *Rawding* lay at anchor in Hampton Roads while efforts were made to find a means of disposing of the coal, which had been loaded at such a high freight that Captain Rickson's flooring and ballast had been removed in order to stow an extra sixty tons. So much for greed. At last a charter was settled to deliver the coal to Martinique.

Captain Torrey's 1940 Voyage · *3*

On this voyage Captain Torrey kept a journal which, I believe, was for the purpose of explaining his actions to investigators should the cargo catch fire, the ship be overlong in her passages, or become involved in warlike activities that might spread from Europe to the French island to which she was bound.[12] It is a document of the frustrations and anxieties that could beset a shipmaster on an ocean voyage in a vessel that was fouled with marine growth, with an indifferent crew, rotten sails, and beset with light winds. Sailing day was 15 June 1940.

No more had he cleared the Virginia Capes than he began to relate his woes: "This is the first time in my life that I was given just time enough to get a crew and stores on board and get to sea before

Captain Winsor W. Torrey works on the deck of the RAWDING, 1940. While the vessel lies at Norfolk, held up with a cargo of coal for Norway, Captain Torrey hews a piece of oak to replace a broken crosstree. Fortunately the defect was discovered before the RAWDING departed. Rot was the constant enemy of wooden ships, and often it lay hidden under many coats of paint. Some mates seldom went aloft to inspect conditions, leaving it to sometimes indifferent crews to spot such problems.
(Courtesy Miner G. Robinson)

At Hampton Roads in 1940, the RAWDING lies at anchor with her lower sails set. The captain has taken the yawl-boat ashore. No doubt the mate has all in readiness to heave in the anchor chain and get underway when the breeze makes up and the captain returns aboard.
(Courtesy Miner G. Robinson)

twelve o'clock p.m. or else. Whether it was insurance or just a bluff I don't know which, whichever it was, they will pay perhaps. This is the worst deal I ever had. Rotten.

"Well here I is and alive and what a day yesterday was. Old Jordan [the cook] after he signed on, went and got drunk and the stores came and he was so drunk he didn't even know they came and everything was thrown in a heap and the crew, part of them, was drunk also." It can be seen that the start of the voyage was far from auspicious.

Once a ship clears the land and takes her departure, the captain begins his sea log and prepares to plot his position by celestial navigation. Captain Torrey had brought his chronometer ashore to have it rated. He soon discovered that it was not properly rated and resorted to his radio receiving set for time ticks and made his own adjustments.

The radio was a battery receiving set and could not transmit, but had both AM and short wave bands. There was so much static on the AM band that it was useless at night, and the captain relied mainly on short wave. On the evening of 20 June he listened to the Joe Louis-Godoy fight, but complained that the short wave was so filled with foreign language broadcasts that even that wasn't very good.

On the same day, one of the sailors was taken ill and the mate had to give him an enema. "I've been going to sea for thirty-nine years," he remarked, "and never had that happen."

The ship was so foul that she would only make about five knots in a fresh breeze. Captain Torrey kept looking aft for sight of the four-master *Helen Barnet Gring*, in which I was sailing. We had sailed a couple of days after the *Rawding* and were making good time on our way from Newport News to Bermuda, with coal, but we were freshly out of the shipyard and had a clean bottom. The *Rawding* did sight another schooner when the Canadian three-master *Daniel Getson* passed by in the opposite direction, bound from Bermuda to Hampton Roads.

The four sailors were all black, and two were aliens with no birth certificates, but most of them had sailed with Torrey's brother, George. The big schooners carried either white or black sailors, depending on a captain's preference or crew availability in a shipping port. American vessels seldom attempted integration, or what sailors called "checkerboard crews." I had sailed in a couple of mixed crews and had no prejudice.

Captain Torrey enjoyed his radio and kept tuned for the war news. One evening he remarked, "Louis got fifty-five thousand dollars last night for the fight—Gee . . . I could buy a schooner for that amount." Another night, " . . . I am waiting for a minister to get through preaching so I can get some time signals again . . . he has just said AMEN. I got 'em 5-25 fast [his chronometer was 5 minutes and 25 seconds fast]."

About this time the ship was moving along with good winds, and the captain remarked that he was getting plenty of sleep . . . no rocks to worry about and no ships to run into. All that could be seen was space and gulfweed.

The mate was keeping the crew busy, and Captain Torrey found little chores to keep himself active. He scraped the coaming and gave it a coat of shellac. Then he cut some stencils from old charts to mark out letters and paint the ship's name on the bows. After he got them painted he found, to his disgust, that he'd forgotten one letter on one side. How lucky it was for the mate or bosun that it hadn't been their doing. Undoubtedly, they had a quiet laugh out of hearing. Perhaps one of them got the task of painting it out and relettering. There is nobody on ship to bawl the captain out.

In latitude 29°04' north and longitude 61°24' west there was little wind, so the captain and mate took turns rowing off in the skiff to take photographs. I know of no other that shows the *Herbert L. Rawding* under full sail.

Although the winds became light, the vessel

While becalmed during the 1940 voyage to the Caribbean, mate Bob Robinson rowed out to take this, the only known photograph of the RAWDING under full sail.
(Courtesy Miner G. Robinson)

kept meandering to the eastward. Only one steamer was sighted during a whole week, and even sharks and dolphin kept away. Captain Torrey wrote: "I can't write all I want to here as I don't know whose hands this might fall into, so just writing something like a log until I arrive in Martinique."

The war news kept getting worse and old Jordan Rector's asthma kept him wheezing in the damp air. One broadcast stated that the British were about to send a lot of civilians to the United States and the U.S. had raised a million dollars to bring them over. "I wonder why they don't take them to Canada?" mused the captain.

On July second the vessel was going fine and headed right down for Martinique, outside of Guadeloupe and the Windward Islands. The sailor who was sick at the start of the voyage was still sick, and the captain wrote: "He is still sick when he has any work to do and has been in his bunk most of the time since I left Norfolk and somebody else has to do his work. He don't know anything anyway, he don't know how to steer or handle a topsail. He is no good in the night anyway."

On July third at 5:00 P.M. the skipper remarked that it was near suppertime and he expected hash, as they'd had salt horse for dinner. He contemplated setting off some torches to celebrate the Fourth but decided they might attract somebody he wouldn't care to see and, on the Fourth, mentioned that they had 580 miles to go. On July fifth he tried out some Coston signals, but didn't like them because they blew out the wrong end.

On the seventh, there was news that France had joined the Germans to fight against England, and a change of course to San Juan, Puerto Rico, was contemplated. However, a later broadcast countered that information. They held on for Mar-

Viewed from aloft, a coal lighter lies alongside the RAWDING at Martinique, 24 July 1940. The coal is hoisted in buckets from the hold and sent down the wooden chute over the rail into the lighters. These sharp but burdensome craft were rowed ashore with long sweeps.
(Courtesy Miner G. Robinson)

tinique and shot a couple of sharks for excitement. There was a big swell rolling, and they tore the foresail and had to lower everything to keep the other sails from slatting to pieces.

In four days the *Rawding* had crept one hundred and eighty miles. The cabin top was leaking, and Torrey did a bit of caulking. He decided to work a little to the eastward. Caulking didn't stop the leaks in the cabin, so he laid canvas over the worst parts.

On July thirteenth the topsails and flying jib were reported torn in a bit of a squall, and that evening they sighted Antigua, the first land sighted in twenty-eight days. On the seventeenth they took a squall and blew the foresail to pieces within sight of Martinique. Before a new foresail could be bent on, they drifted to leeward, and the disgusted skipper wrote, "It will take us two days to get back again."

At 5:30 P.M. on the eighteenth there was nothing but bad news. He had sailed her all the way back to Dominica to get to windward again. They had been within seventeen miles of Fort-de-France two nights before, and "1:00 P.M. The laceline on the spanker broke, so had to get that down and reeve off a new one. All four topsails have been torn. The fore has been down on deck, the mizzen is still on the masthead, torn, so it can't be used and nothing, only knitting twine to sew with. Have used 6 balls of twine sewing sails. It takes these guys so long to do anything at all . . . ."

Presumably the *Rawding* arrived in Fort-de-France the next day. Here Captain Torrey's journal of the outward passage ended. One can imagine his frustrations, sailing a foul-bottomed vessel in fickle winds, with rotten sails, a leaky cabin, and a crew he could not depend on. To add to his worries were the uncertainties of an approaching war. He had little faith that his owners would handle things efficiently on their end or even whether the authorities at Fort-de-France would give him a friendly reception, since France had already surrendered to Germany. French temperament and bureaucracy can be difficult, even in normal times, and Captain Torrey could hardly have looked forward to his encounter with officialdom under the circumstances.

It has always bothered me when academic historians claim that the best shipmasters left sail at the end of the clipper ship era and either retired or shipped in steam. Their main claim to fame was the fact that they aggressively sought it at a tremendous cost in human lives, strained hulls, broken spars, and tattered sails, on new vessels with the best of gear and huge crews. To be sure, some of those masters were gentlemen both ashore and afloat and were consummate seamen at the

same time. Others were egomaniacs who allowed their mates to turn the main deck into a perpetual combat zone, where they broke both bodies and spirits. Many such retired ashore and became pillars of the church and community, where they were often as much feared as respected. The later, big down-easters bred some vicious specimens, but also there were masters who sailed round the world with contented crews who probably produced more work than sullen men who were little more than slaves.

By the time the large coasting schooner appeared on the scene there were laws restricting the use of force. The sailing ship did not breed soft men nor tolerate incompetence in its masters or mates. These men learned to command through force of character. Some bore a rough exterior and were profane; others were quiet and kindly in manner but always maintained a bearing that told the most unruly sailor he was at risk if he tried to get out of hand.

Captain Winsor Torrey was the latter sort of man, and during four voyages with him I saw him sail a leaky old four-master through fog, gales, and snow, with happy crews who had complete confidence in his ability to navigate the rocky coasts of Maine and Nova Scotia. He was a man who could crack a joke with the helmsman, even take the wheel for a while to let him run forward for a cup of hot coffee on a cold day, but one never essayed familiarity with him. He could not crack on sail, for the schooners in my days were old survivors with old sails and gear; they were run with utmost economy, and a serious accident meant another vessel hauled up in the mud to rot, for costly repairs could not be recovered. It took a good man to keep such a craft afloat and earning her way.

After arrival at Fort-de-France, the *Rawding*

was towed around to the weather shore of Martinique to discharge her coal. From there, she sailed down to Aruba and loaded goat manure for Baltimore. Captain Torrey left no record of the happenings from arrival at Martinique until sailing from Aruba, but one affair I do remember.

One morning, while at Aruba, one of the sailors was found dead in his bunk. I presume this was the one who had so much stomach trouble and was little use about the deck. Bob was very much annoyed that the Dutch authorities required the body to be prepared for burial aboard ship. The black crew would have nothing to do with touching their erstwhile shipmate, so Bob and the engineer for the donkey engine prepared the body. The captain was annoyed at the red tape and expense, and few tears were shed for the deceased. Sailors are not supposed to die aboard ship. At sea it is a simple matter to slip them over the side, but in port it just makes a nuisance and more work for all hands. In the hot weather of the tropics, such matters are disposed of quickly, and another man was shipped for the passage home.

It wasn't until September eleventh that the ship finished loading at Aruba, was prepared for sea, and began dragging her cargo of "goat" and bottom-load of barnacles northward. I'm afraid much of the romance of the sea was lost upon her crew as she drifted up past Haiti, through Windward and Crooked Island passages, and passed out by San Salvador. There was a battle with cockroaches over who was to eat the potatoes, and one sailor was stung by a scorpion. The sails were constantly being repaired, the winds were light and often ahead. They saw a few steamers and one three-master, the *Frank S. Morey*.

On 9 October the vessel had finally worked her way up to Hatteras, but that locality lived up to its name and a nor'easter had the *Rawding* running before it for a while, and later hove to under easy sail for another day. It wasn't until 16 October that they passed in by Cape Henry. The Norfolk pilot boat came alongside, but Captain Torrey couldn't get a Baltimore pilot and decided to sail up without one. By this time he was tired of the voyage and disgusted with his crew. One notation was: "Noon. Have the topsail all ready to set and now will keep that guy up there until he gets it set. I have to do everything they make such a time doing nothing."

The wind was still light and the vessel crept up Chesapeake Bay, anchoring when the tide set ahead and getting under way on the flood until, at 7:30 A.M. on 23 October, there is the following notation in the journal:

7:30 A.M. There she is, anchored off Baltimore Light; so that ends this trip. 42 days from Auba. What a record!

10:25 A.M. I don't know what the matter is with Foss or Sides [the managing owners] the reason they haven't paid attention to business and had a tug boat to pick me up after I arrived here. Maybe they want me to sail up this channel, but I'm not going to. I have sailed 141 miles up this bay with no pilot and I'm through saving tow bills for them. I've been up all night and what do I get? Nothing! They can take the *Rawding* and go to hell or do anything they want with her. I can't understand why a tug hasn't been down before this. Gosh, I'd like to get up there and docked before night and get some grub to eat. I'm tired of eating beans all the time.

With these words, Captain Torrey ended his journal and his last ocean voyage in one of the large schooners that had been so much a part of his life since boyhood.

My First Voyage in the *Herbert L. Rawding*, 1940-1941 · 4

Meanwhile, I had knocked about in various ships and places and had been shipwrecked in the *Helen Barnet Gring* on Cayo Verde on the north coast of Cuba. After being shipped home, I was spending a quiet week or so with my mother in Vermont when I received a telegram from Baltimore asking if I would ship as bosun in the *Rawding*. I wasn't long getting my gear packed, and looked forward to being shipmates with mate Bob Robinson and Captain Torrey again. By train and steamer I made my way to Norfolk, soon had my gear aboard, and went to work.[13]

Captain Rickson came down to spend a few days aboard and bought a big turkey for our Thanksgiving Day dinner. Shortly after the turkey came aboard and Captain Rickson had departed for his hotel, Captain Torrey regaled us with the story of the turkey. The afternoon before the festive occasion, Captain Rickson asked Captain Torrey what was planned for Thanksgiving dinner. Captain Torrey replied that it would probably be pot roast.

"POT ROAST!" shouted Captain Rickson. "Who the hell ever heard of a goddam pot roast for Thanksgiving? Get your goddam hat and we'll go buy a turkey."

"We walked up the street until we came to a market and went in. There were a couple of women at the counter and we had to wait. Rickson sidled over near the counter and stared at a turkey displayed there. When the ladies turned to go, the market man asked Rickson what he could do for him.

"Well, I want a goddam turkey," said Rickson, "but I don't want that damn thing you've got there. That's so sharp, if you turned it upside down and put a sail on it, the damn thing could sail three points off the wind. I want a turkey with some beam to it. It's got to feed nine hungry men."

We finished our repairs, towed over to Newport News, and took on a full cargo of coal for Pointe-à-Pitre, Guadeloupe. That evening, while still at the dock, Bob came to my room and told me that both he and Captain Torrey had been fired. Captain Mitchell C. Decker, formerly of the *Edward L. Swan*, was to go as master and would bring his own mate. I was both angry and upset enough to say that I would go with them, but they talked me into staying. I never discovered why these two men were fired. They were the finest sort of seamen and shipmates, but I presume owners have the right to hire their own men.

Captain Mitchell C. Decker poses with Mrs. Decker on Easter Sunday, 1944. At this time Captain Decker had left sail to command merchant steamships transporting war supplies to Europe. (Courtesy Captain Mitchell C. Decker)

Captain Decker arrived the next day and brought Captain Berne Bradford as mate. Captain Decker was a fine shipmaster and had unlimited masters licenses in both sail and steam, but preferred sailing vessels if he could find one, since he could carry family members and Mrs. Decker enjoyed sailing with him.

I remember his telling me that he had started his seagoing career in fishing schooners and then went on in schooners in the West Indies trade. At one time he took several new three-masters out of Liverpool, Nova Scotia, on voyages to the Gulf of Mexico. One of these, the *Annie*, provided more than enough excitement. The vessel was floundering around in light airs in the Gulf one morning. There were several waterspouts in the distance, but

Captain Decker was not much concerned. The cook called out that breakfast was ready. Telling the man at the wheel to keep his eyes open, he went below. In a few minutes the man at the wheel called out that one spout was coming nearer. Captain Decker replied that he would be up in a minute. Again the helmsman called out that the spout was coming quite close. The captain decided to have a look. He had no more than reached the deck than, with a frightful roar, the waterspout burst upon them, threw the vessel on its beam ends, burst open the hatches and she began to fill. Mrs. Decker and her baby, Louise, were trapped in the cabin. The only means of escape was through one of the small cabin windows. Mrs. Decker managed to clamber up and push the baby out, but try as they would, they could not get Mrs. Decker through.

Meanwhile, the yawl boat slung over the stern had been lowered into the water. One of the sailors spotted a can of engine oil and passed it up. Stripping off her clothes, Mrs. Decker poured oil all over her body, the men pulled with a will, and the captain's naked wife slid through the opening.

"I was too scared to be embarrassed," Mrs. Decker told me. "One of the men gave me his pants and another his shirt. We were several days in the boat before being picked up." The vessel foundered.

Mr. Bradford was a short, wirey, little fellow in his sixties. He came from Maine and had at one time been champion lightweight boxer of that state. Over the years Mr. Bradford had kept himself in great physical shape; he neither smoked nor drank alcohol, tea, or coffee. He was a mild-mannered fellow all the time I knew him, but there were legends that he was a veritable tiger if the need arose. He had sailed in a number of three-masted schooners in the coastwise and West Indies trades and later was a tugboat captain in New York Harbor. He wished to make one more trip in sail and then retire.

Mr. Everett Bean was donkey engineer. "Chief" was always the title for the engineer aboard ship. Mr. Bean had been some years in the *Edna Hoyt* and came to the *Rawding* after the *Hoyt* was lost. He was a placid old fellow who kept his head completely shaved, had a huge belly, and could consume beer in unbelievable quantity. When discharging cargo he would sit at his controls with a case of beer and a couple of bottles of wine arranged about him. Perspiration would run down his face, and his T-shirt would be soaked, but he would always have steam and could land a bucket of coal or a pallet of glassware on an egg without breaking it. At sea there was no beer, but at any time of day or night one only had to ring the engine room bell and almost instantaneously there would be power.

In the forecastle, we had three black seamen and a little Portuguese fellow who was practically shanghaied aboard, to his dismay.

It was after dark one night when the little "Portugee" came aboard. I was below and heard voices that sounded like someone alongside. Coming on deck, I found a launch at the ladder and heard an exchange:

"This don't look like no barge to me."

"Well this is the *Herbert L. Rawding*. This is the vessel I was told to bring you to."

"Hey, are you the mate?" the launchman called as I looked down over the side. "I've got a man for you. Send down a line for his gear."

I sent down the line, hauled it up, and looked at the curly-headed little fellow who followed it up.

"Hey, this ain't no barge is it?"

"No, this is a schooner."

"I ain't shippin' on this thing," he shouted.

"Hey, come back," he yelled at the departing launch. There was no reply as the launch putted away into the dark.

"Take your gear forward," I said, and noted the dark forms of the other sailors gathered outside the forecastle. As he scuttled forward, I wondered why the skipper had hired him and what sort of reception he would receive. Schoonermen were hard to find, now that unions had come into power. Life was easy in steam, the quarters were better, there were three watches; the pay was three times as much and seldom a cry for "All Hands!" in the middle of a storm-tossed night. There were old sailors who knew no other way than the sailing ship. There were a few "nuts" like myself, who thought life in sail was wonderful. Our new recruit was neither of these.

Consideration should probably be given to the fact that Manny had never been in a sailing vessel, that he had been shipped under somewhat false pretenses, and that he suddenly found himself in a forecastle with three black men who were competent seamen and probably resented him. Poor Manny may have been able to steer a barge behind a towboat, but had none of the attributes of a good sailor.

With about 1,900 tons of coal in the hold, the *Herbert L. Rawding* had been towed out to Hampton Roads and anchored. There we cleaned up the mess left over from loading. Coal had spilled over from the hatches and she was covered with coal dust from one end to the other. Strong-backs were placed in the hatches, covers laid across, three layers of tarpaulins were laid over each hatch and battened down on the sides; hatch bars were laid down over all, one to a side on each hatch, and bolted securely. Next, the hose was broken out and the whole ship received a saltwater washing and scrubbing. It was also necessary to check the shrouds and take up or slack off on turnbuckles, as old wooden ships had a tendency to hog up when light and straighten out with cargo aboard.

Captain Decker seemed to have a lot of things to take care of ashore, and we found plenty of work to occupy the crew for a few days. Once the sail covers dried out, we folded and stowed them away. The cook's locker was filled with coal, some new lines were rove off, and a new topsail was bent on. Ships setting off to cross the Gulf Stream in December are well advised to prepare for the worst.

While anchored at Newport News, 10 December 1940, the author photographed the last gathering of three active four-masted schooners. From the deck of the HERBERT L. RAWDING, the ALBERT F. PAUL is seen in the foreground, and the ANNA R. HEIDRITTER in the background. All three vessels are loaded with coal, the PAUL bound for Bermuda and the RAWDING and HEIDRITTER for Guadeloupe. The film was subsequently damaged by moisture during the voyage.
(Photo by author)

Two other four-masters loaded coal and towed out to anchor near us. The *Anna R. Heidritter* was also bound for Point-à-Pitre and the *Albert F. Paul* for Bermuda. On an anchorage that had often seen forty or fifty big schooners swinging to their hooks, this was the last time three four-masters ever anchored together.

In December 1940, those three old schooners represented a good proportion of the four-masted schooners left on the Atlantic Coast. The *Helen Barnet Gring* had been wrecked, the *J.S. Clise* had been towed in, waterlogged, and the *Annie C. Ross* had been laid up in Newtown Creek, Brooklyn, never to sail again. Two old vessels had been resurrected: the former four-masted barkentine *Reine Marie Stewart*, and the *Constellation*, formerly the *Sally Persis Noyes*, would sail on unfinished war time voyages under the American flag. The *Theoline* made one more trip and was wrecked. In Canada, two former American four-masters were still sailing: the *Lillian E. Kerr* and *James E. Newsom*. Both were later lost during the war.

There was nothing pathetic about this trio of schooners; though they were old, they were well kept and seaworthy. The *Heidritter* was the oldest of the lot, having been built as the *Cohasset* in 1903, a double-decked vessel of 965 gross tons. About 1910 a disastrous fire destroyed the upper part of the vessel; she was rebuilt with a single deck and registered a mere 694 gross tons. So complete was her rebuilding that not only was her name changed, but also her official number and signal letters. For some years Edward L. Swan was listed as her owner and probably retained a large part of her, though at this time she was registered under Anna R. Heidritter Corporation. Captain Bennett D. Coleman was part owner and master from 1925 until her loss in 1942.

The *Albert F. Paul* had been built in 1917 for C.C. Paul & Company of Baltimore, and was still under their ownership. The *Paul* had always been well maintained and busy in the coasting and West Indies trades. She was commanded for many years by Captain Robert O. Jones, a man who had lost a leg in an accident and stumped around on an artificial one.

There seemed to be some possibility of a race between the *Heidritter* and ourselves, but she and the *Paul* weighed anchor a couple of days before we got away. Early one morning we heard their gasoline hoisting engines popping away, heard the clank of pawls as chain was hove in, and saw the huge lower sails gradually hoisted. As their anchors broke loose, the headsails were quickly hoisted, they swung away on their courses and faded from sight, bound for Cape Henry and the open sea.

We took stores aboard from a boat owned by Wm. H. Swan & Sons. There were barrels of salt beef, salt pork, cod tongues and sounds, salt mackerel, a couple of smoked shoulders, potatoes, cabbage, carrots, turnips, and onions. There were also canned goods, such as peas, beans, corn, beets, fruits, and canned meat. Always there was plenty of curry powder and rice. Old African Sam, our cook, liked hominy, so we often had that for breakfast. American schooners fed well and plenty. Though we ate fresh meat in port, it would last only a few days after we sailed. An icebox was the best a schooner could offer for refrigeration.

Eventually, Captain Decker cleared up whatever problems were keeping us at anchor, or the weather provided the incentive. We finally hove up anchor and headed for Guadeloupe. It was Friday, 13 December 1940, and some of our crew were most unhappy about the date. Regardless of growling, dawn came in with a light southerly breeze, and preparations were made to get under way. Halyards were led to the winches and, beginning with the spanker, the sails were slowly hoisted and trimmed in flat; first the spanker, then the mizzen, main, and foresail. Meanwhile, the anchor was slowly hove in, the mate watching its progress on the forecastle head, while I tended the sails. The little Portugee was sent below to stow the anchor chain, one man tended the hose to wash mud off the anchor chain, two men took the staysail and jib halyards to winch heads, while I tended the downhauls and watched to see that everything was clear. Captain Decker stood by the wheel and called out when he felt the throat and peak halyards were high enough; we stopped them off and belayed them, then began hoisting the next sail. In the engine room the chief maintained steam and the exhaust huffed and puffed as the winches turned.

When the chain was hove short (straight up and down) the mate called out "Anchor short, sir."

Captain Decker replied, "O.K. Break her out and get the headsails on her."

The windlass slowed as the whole weight of the chain and an anchor buried in the mud came upon it. The huff and puff of the engine slowed. One could feel the mighty strain as it strove to pull the anchor clear. Suddenly, as the puffing increased in speed, one knew instinctively the anchor had come away.

"Hoist away the headsails," called out the captain.

The staysail and jib, with their tailropes hauled to weather, billowed out and rose on their stays. The vessel's head began to fall to leeward and she slowly gathered way. As soon as the staysail and jib were secured, we set the flying and outer jibs. By this time we were moving through the anchored shipping, making a course for Lynnhaven Roads and the open sea. The mud-coated anchor had been brought to water's edge and left to hang while the mate took a hand in getting the headsails set and properly sheeted home. Since the *Rawding* had patent anchors, there was no need to go through the lengthy process of catting and securing it. It was only necessary to clean it of mud, make certain there was no twist in the chain, and heave it, carefully, into the hawsepipe.

Along the decks lay a seemingly impossible clutter of heaped ropes to be cleared away and properly coiled, each in its place. Sheets, halyards, topping lifts, boom tackles, sail stops, and other gear had been dropped and had to be put in the proper locations. Captain Decker gave us a chance to accomplish this work and, as the breeze continued to hold, gave orders to set the topsails. Three sailors sprang aloft to cast off gaskets and get the topsails ready to be stretched. Our new recruit had no idea of what was going on, so was kept on deck to pull or slack, as might be needed. By the time we cleared Cape Henry, the *Rawding* was dressed in her four lowers, four topsails, and four headsails, everything in her wardrobe, and she must have been a picture to those fortunate enough to see her.

We had visions of a wonderful start on our voyage, but soon after clearing Cape Henry, the wind eased off. Night fell and the shore lights remained visible. Next morning we could still make out the dim outline of the shore.

As we had left the Virginia Capes and taken our departure, the watches were set. Mr. Bradford had Willoughby Banks, a black fellow from Trinidad, and Manny in his watch. I was given a fine black fellow named Squashie and Joe, a very black seaman from Brava, Cape Verde Islands. Both men in my watch had been in sailing vessels before I was born. I don't know whether Squashie had sailed in other than schooners, but Joe had been in square-rigged whalers and merchant ships as well as schooners. The Cape Verde Islands are Portuguese and have sent forth many fine seamen.

In large schooners the bosun was expected to be sort of an acting second mate. He took charge of the captain's (or starboard) watch and, while not expected to be a navigator, was expected to perform the deck-keeping duties of a mate. I had already made one voyage as mate of a schooner and felt capable of handling men and making decisions. Like many another young fellow, I was to discover that I had not learned it all.

Late in the day a breeze sprang up from the southwest, but it backed around to southeast before morning, with rain, fresh winds, and squalls. The topsails were furled, the spanker lowered, and the outer and flying jibs taken in. Under close-hauled fore, main, mizzen, and two headsails, we lay into the wind while the seas washed at will across our deep-laden decks.

Life at sea can be somewhat miserable in such weather. Though the wind was strong, it was not gale velocity. The seas were choppy, but they were not the huge rolling greybeard type which roar out of a full-fledged storm. The southerly wind and rain were comparatively warm, but still, after four hours on deck in such weather, a fellow is glad to start the watch below.

The officer's quarters on a large schooner were quite luxurious compared to the cramped quarters of the sailors in the forecastle, with its plain painted walls and board slatted bunks and plain, cotton-filled mattresses. The cabins were finished entirely in panelled wood which the overworked cook was expected to keep bright in his spare hours. The master's quarters consisted of a large

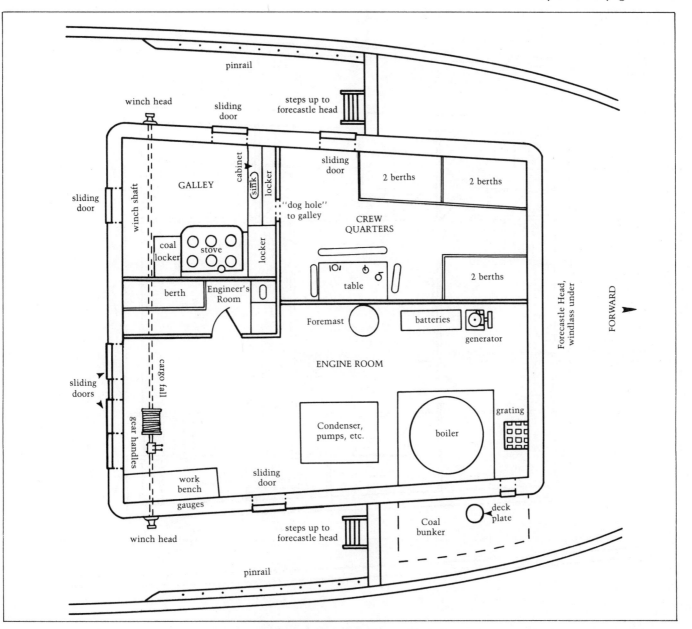

Layout of the *Rawding*'s forward house,
as remembered by the author.
Drawn by Bill Gill.

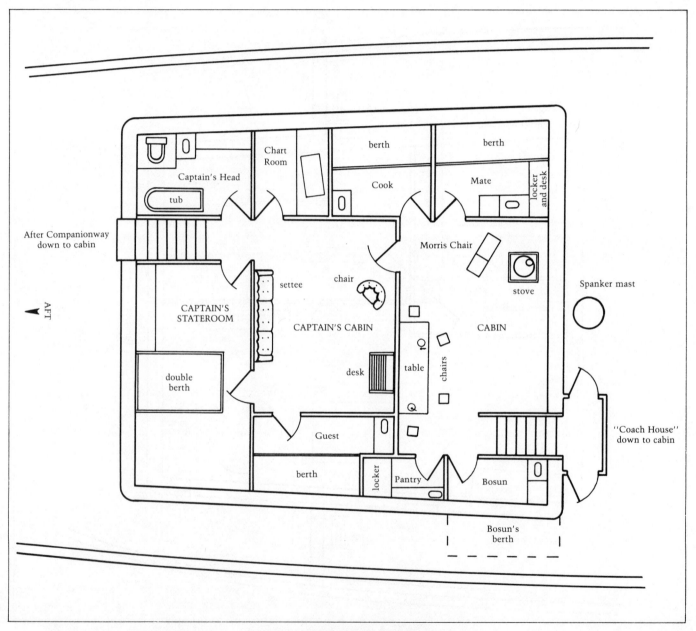

Layout of the *Rawding*'s after house,
as remembered by the author.
Drawn by Bill Gill.

saloon, one or two spare rooms, a chart room, a bath, and his own large stateroom, which usually contained a double bed, a desk, and possibly a couple of chairs. This section of the cabin generally occupied better than half the house. Forward in the house was a large room used for dining, with either a folding or stationary table at which all the officers ate. On the port side of the *Rawding* were the cook's and mate's rooms, while on the starboard side were the pantry, the forward companionway, and, tucked away in the side of the vessel, the bosun's room.

While the designer of the *Rawding* might have believed in fairly comfortable quarters for mates and cooks, he displayed an utter contempt for any convenience the bosun might desire. My room was hardly more than six feet long. When I stood up I could almost touch both walls with my elbows. The bunk was tucked in under the deck between the side of the cabin and the rail, so any traffic from the wheel forward along the starboard side was directly over my head. Above the bunk was one porthole that had to be kept closed in any kind of sea when the vessel was deeply loaded, because water was constantly swashing along the deck just outside.

When I lay in the bunk I could touch the overhead by drawing up my legs. On top of these discomforts, I was forced to wage a constant war with a battalion of bedbugs which not only felt that they shared equal rights to my quarters, but also demanded my blood as rental. When the complete history of the sea is written, I hope historians will not omit the vermin that were the constant companions of seamen through all their trials and misfortunes, as well as their successes.

All in all, there was not too much to complain of in the *Rawding*. The vessel was in excellent condition. Her rigging was good and the weather was about what one might reasonably expect. We didn't have much more than a day of nasty weather before the wind returned to the southeast. In short order we passed into the beautiful, clear waters of the Gulf Stream, with its patches of yellow gulfweed, dainty pink and blue Portuguese men-o-war, flying fish, and billowing white clouds that flattened out to a dirty gray on the bottom and poured a few buckets of water over the vessel from time to time.

We bore up on a course to the northward of Bermuda, for a sailing vessel bound to the Leeward Islands always tried to get as far to the east as possible before getting down to the region of the northeast trades. The westerly winds prevail north of Bermuda at most times of the year; therefore a sailing vessel tries to get as far east as possible to take advantage of the trades when she has worked into their latitude. The northeast trades farther south do not always live up to their name and, sometimes, have a disconcerting way of coming from a bit south of east. A vessel getting too far to leeward can be a long time reaching port.

Unfortunately we did not hold our westerly wind for long. Soon it swung around to the eastward and, with the vessel hauled up on the port tack, we were forced to pass somewhat to the southward of Bermuda. We shoved along our way with all sails set, as beautiful a sight as the eye could see, but day after day the only eyes to see us were the eyes of those on board and those of the sea birds. The sailing ship travels a lonely path upon the ocean. Occasionally she may cross a steamship lane, but her road is the lane of the open sea, wherever the wind may direct.

Even latter-day sailing vessels traveled without wireless. Many a schooner has met her end in these waters with only the wind, the sea, the birds, and the fish to know her fate. The only epitaph of many a schooner reads like this one: "The schooner *Doris Hamlin*. Missing since February, 1940, bound from Norfolk for Las Palmas." Such is the last known record of a four-masted schooner lost in the same year of the *Rawding's* voyage I relate. I had been offered a berth in the *Doris Hamlin*, but was otherwise employed.

We encountered remarkably good weather. Daytime watches were spent in tarring down the rigging, some little sail patching and possibly a bit of painting. Official day started at 4:00 A.M. when the cook was called to make coffee for the morning watch. It was tough to have to turn out after only four hours below. The man at the wheel would gaze with drooping eyes at the compass, and the man on lookout would pace back and forth on the forecastle head, trying to work the sleep from his bones lest he succumb to the desire to seat himself on the forward edge of the house for a moment, an act that invariably meant dropping off to sleep and a possible call-down from the mate on watch.

First, the smell of wood smoke coming from the galley stack, then the smell of soft coal added to the fire and, at last, the heavenly aroma of boiling coffee would herald the cook's efforts with the coffee pot. When the brew was ready, the lookout would go to the galley door, pour out a steaming cup of coffee, lather a couple of pilot biscuits with butter, and soon feel as if life had begun again. Finished with his coffee, he would relieve the man at the wheel, who would proceed forward. Captains were notoriously absent at this ungodly hour of the day, but might put in an appearance if conditions favored a star sight as the sky began to brighten and a horizon promised to show itself.

If there was sufficient light, ships work began about 6:00 A.M. in good weather. The hose was usually broken out and the decks washed down with salt water to keep the seams from drying out under the heat of the tropic sun.

At 8:00 A.M. the forenoon watch would begin whatever had been lined up for the day, and this work would generally be continued by the afternoon watch, who would work right up until the first dog-watch came on deck at 4:00 P.M. and continue until the first sitting for supper at 5:00 P.M.

Although the procedure varied from ship to ship, aboard some American schooners it was the custom in the first dog-watch for one man to take the wheel and the other finish up what had been left undone by the afternoon watch, and put tools away. At 5:00 P.M. the cook would call out that supper was ready. The watch below would be joined by the spare man on deck, who would eat and then relieve the man at the wheel. This meant that all meals were finished by 6:00 P.M., when the second dog-watch came on deck. Some captains insisted that the watch on deck stay on deck and eat a cold supper at four bells. I don't believe they gained much by this tactic as the sailors were not overly zealous and the poor, overworked cook had an hour added to his long day.

The second dog-watch, from 6:00 P.M., was never worked. One man took the wheel, while the other took it easy. If the weather was warm, it was common for the fellows in the watch below to sit on deck and yarn. They would be up and ready when eight bells came and they would take over until midnight.

With a good mate planning the work there was little idle time during the day, even in good weather. There was always something to do aboard a ship. The crews might grumble when kept busy all watch, but, as any good mate knows, a busy crew is a happy crew and a well-kept vessel instills an "esprit de corps" among crewmen that helps immeasurably when the going gets tough and there is a need for all hands to work long and hard for survival of the ship or to save her gear.

Our passage to Guadeloupe was about as uneventful as any I ever made. With the exception of Manny, who claimed he was unable to go aloft and thus shifted an extra burden upon his crewmates, we had a good crew. Some of the crews I sailed with would have thrown such a fellow as Manny out of the forecastle and made his life miserable. For some reason that gang gave him an easy time, although they certainly let him know what they thought of him. There were times when I wished he'd been able to get back aboard the launch that brought him to us.

The wind constantly hung to the eastward, and we kept the vessel "full and by" for practically the whole passage, in an effort to make as much easting as possible. The horse latitudes were kind to us and we had only a few days of the usual calms and light airs. Then we were into the trades, which still had little of their northerly slant and forced us to keep our sheets trimmed in.

Christmas passed with little to mark it, except for a better meal than usual and the fact that no ship's work was done other than man the wheel and handle whatever sail was necessary.

The skipper had a battery-powered radio in the cabin. Ordinarily, we would have heard little of the news from him, but during that year, 1940, there were stirring events in which all persons took a serious interest. Each evening, after listening to one of the broadcasts, the skipper came on deck to pass the latest news on to the officer of the watch and, naturally, to the man at the wheel. Thus we were aware of current events, an innovation but recently introduced to sailing vessels, and one

which I quietly regretted. Before the introduction of receiving sets we sailed in a world of our own. There was plenty in our daily life of enough interest to make up conversation, and many a watch below was spent yarning about other vessels and other trips we had made or heard about. These things were of much greater interest than the goings-on in the world we had left.

On the evening of our seventeenth day we picked up land to leeward, and daylight found us running down between Marie-Galante and Guadeloupe, then up the bay and to anchorage off Pointe-à-Pitre, during the forenoon of New Year's Day, 1941.

As soon as Pointe-à-Pitre was sighted, we began casting around for sight of the *Anna R. Heidritter's* topmasts. She had left Newport News so far ahead of us we were certain we would find her awaiting our arrival and be half discharged. The skipper's first question, when the pilot came aboard, was whether anything had been heard of the other vessel. The pilot had heard nothing. We had seen nothing of her during our own passage, so it had not been much of a race. Now that we knew we had beaten her time, our jubilation was tinged with concern for her well-being.

Pointe-à-Pitre was loosely blockaded at that time. The French West Indies had declared for the Vichy government. There was a French naval training cruiser lying there and the British were keeping an eye on the port in an effort to keep her from getting out for use by the Germans. It was a pleasant little port to lie in, with only small native craft displaying much activity and an occasional steamer dropping in from the United States.

We stripped our gaffs and rigged them for discharging, took off our hatch covers, and waited to get rid of our cargo. I don't believe more than two lighters came alongside for coal in the first week. The skipper made a trip ashore each day to see what could be done to hurry things up. Each afternoon he returned with a few new remarks about Frenchmen in general and about Frenchmen on Guadeloupe in particular.

The fact that we were not getting discharged did not mean that the crew of the *Rawding* had time to be idle. We sent the men aloft in bosun chairs to scrape down the topmasts and paint trucks and mastheads. When that was done we rigged the triangle, where three men could sit, and scraped down the lower masts. The *Rawding* was a fine looking vessel at any time, but with her masts all freshly scraped and slushed, and her trucks and mastheads gleaming in their new coat of white paint to set off the gray of her hull, she was a handsome sight, lying there in the bay.

When Manny was handed a bosun chair and ordered aloft to scrape a topmast, he refused to go, with the excuse that he suffered from hemorrhoids and couldn't sit in the chair. I took my problem to Captain Decker, who soon had Manny in a boat, bound for shore and an examination by a doctor. Manny was left in the waiting room while captain and doctor consulted. Eventually, Manny was invited to the examination room, ordered to strip off his clothes for examination, and noted the doctor laying out a formidable array of wicked looking instruments. With a malevolent scowl, the doctor picked out the largest knife in his collection and ordered Manny to bend over. The terrified Manny capitulated in haste. That afternoon he was high aloft and scraping with a will.

About a week after our arrival at Pointe-à-Pitre I spotted four topmasts looming up across the land at the harbor entrance. The *Anna R. Heidritter* soon hove into sight. Though she had left well

The ANNA R. HEIDRITTER lies at anchor at Las Piedras, Venezuela, February 1941. In the foreground a local lighter drops its sail as it comes alongside the RAWDING with a load of "goatina." (Photo by author)

before us, she had gotten off to leeward and had to beat her way up against the trade winds. She had been a full month on the passage, where we had been only eighteen days. It was good to see her show up at last. We knew men aboard her and had grown apprehensive as day after day passed with no word of her safety.

True to their policy, the Frenchmen gave the *Heidritter* an immediate discharge, so again she sailed about five days ahead of us; this time for Las Piedras, Venezuela, for which port we were also bound. We expected to arrive at Las Piedras and find that she had loaded and already departed.

As soon as the last lighter departed for shore, we weighed anchor and set off for Venezuela. With a fair wind to drive us on our way we sped along. Down into the hold we went, to shovel up the last dregs of coal. That which could be used by the "chief" we put in the bunkers, the sweepings went over the side. It probably took us about five days to reach Las Piedras, sailing down past Curaçao and Aruba, then swinging south into the Gulf of Venezuela. Las Piedras lies in the lee on the west shore of the Paraguanà Peninsula.

Upon arrival at Las Piedras we were amazed to find the *Anna R. Heidritter* lying at anchor. What was more surprising was the fact that her sides were high out of the water, an indication that she had little, if any, cargo aboard. Captain Decker, being an old hand in those waters, lost no time making his way ashore. It transpired that the authorities had demanded that Captain Coleman of the *Heidritter* turn his ship's papers over to them while the ship was being loaded. This the captain had refused to do. There was no American consul in the area, and the situation was deadlocked.

Viewed from the quarterdeck, several lighters lie along the RAWDING's port side. Stagings are hung over the side as bags of "goat" are passed aboard. In the distance is the bleak shore of the Paraguana Peninsula of Venezuela.
(Photo by author)

Captain Decker got in touch with General Leon Jurado, the political boss of the area, and soon had things set straight. At the same time, he used his friendship to get the jump on Captain Coleman. This time the *Rawding* filled her hold, while the *Heidritter* saw us fade away in the distance.

The Paraguanà Peninsula is a barren piece of real estate, with little vegetation except cactus and sage brush. It is inhabited by a few Indians and thousands of goats. These goats were primarily used for their skins, but, many years before, Captain Harold G. Foss had discovered there was a valuable byproduct. All those goats produced thousands of tons of manure that could be utilized by fertilizer plants in the United States. Captain Foss and General Jurado took advantage of this, and shiploads of "goatina" were shipped north each year. The firm of Foss and Crabtree held a monopoly on this trade.

I had been to Las Piedras the previous summer, when we loaded the *Helen Barnet Gring* with "goatina," and lost both ship and cargo on the north coast of Cuba. There was nothing to attract me ashore, so I remained aboard the whole time we were loading.

Stages were rigged over the side, and small sailing craft brought the cargo out in burlap bags, which were passed up the side by hand and carried to the hatch, slit open, and dumped below. Down in the hold a horde of Indians worked in the dust, trimming the cargo back from the hatchways and levelling it off. It was a hot, dusty, and thoroughly unpleasant job. These natives worked for a few cents a day, and were a poverty-stricken group of humans who would beg and search the slop bucket for scraps of bread or meat the cook might be throwing out.

It took about two weeks to load 1,600 tons of cargo. We put on the hatch covers, squared away, and left the *Anna R. Heidritter* to follow us for a change.

Running off before the northwest gale in March 1941, the RAWDING sets only the standing jib. Sailors called this "running off with dry decks," in spite of the fact that the tops of seas continually slopped through the rails. Photographs do not give an accurate impression of the height of the seas as they towered over the stern, then swept by under the vessel.
(Photo by author)

The *Rawding* must have been a beautiful sight as she worked her way up past Haiti, through the Windward and Crooked Island passages, with light and fitful airs. We had enjoyed our two and a half months in the tropics and wished we could leave a month later, for this voyage would bring us on the coast in early March, a month notorious for westerly gales.

Off San Salvador we picked up a strong, easterly half-gale, with rain and a moderate sea. This swept us along for forty-eight hours with topsails and outer jib tied up and the vessel knocking off a steady nine knots. We felt well on the way to a flying passage home when, suddenly, the wind died out, leaving us in long, oily swells left by the deserting wind. The vessel rolled idly on the empty sea.

Next morning the sun rose red in a hazy sky. It beat down in tropical fury all the forenoon, blistering fresh paint and making tar in the rigging bubble. The old vessel rolled easily and stayed within sight of a great patch of weeds for hours.

During the afternoon a light breeze sprang up astern, gradually freshening and hauling into the southwest as evening approached. All four topsails were set again and, with the wind on her port quarter, the *Rawding* began to step along on the road home.

That evening when I came on deck to take over the eight to twelve watch, Captain Decker was pacing back and forth, looking at the topsails swelling overhead and pondering whether the wind would hold all evening.

"Glass is going down," he remarked before going below. "Wouldn't be surprised if it might haul a bit to the north. Be sure to give me a call if it breezes up."

It was a grand night for sailing. I stood on the weather side keeping an eye on the sails, watching the sea for a sign of another ship, feeling the life in her as she heeled to the press of the wind, watching the phosphorescent wake reel out like a wide silver ribbon astern. The glow from the binnacle made the dark face of the negro helmsman stand out in bold relief as he put his shoulders into the effort of giving the vessel a little "up helm" to keep her off the wind. He eased a few spokes back when her head showed signs of swinging.

As the skipper predicted, the wind began to haul forward a bit when I had been on deck about an hour. I called the lookout down from the forecastle head, turned out the chief, led a messenger line back from the winch to the halyards, and we hove in the sheets a bit. The wind was nearly abeam and freshening all the time and the vessel lay farther over. The wash from her lee seemed to fly by.

"This," I thought "is real sailing. I'll see what the old girl will do when she has a chance."

I saw what the old girl would do. She would do about ten knots with all sail set, a moderate sea and a good, strong wind on the beam. She laid her rail right down to the water and acted as though she actually was making about twenty-one knots. This was the sort of sailing I went to sea for. I wouldn't call the skipper unless it breezed up a little more, although I knew if he were on deck he would be taking in the topsails. I figured if I could hold on until midnight we would take them in with the help of the other watch and then let them tie them up. I was a little disturbed by an occasional flash of lightning that showed far to the northwest, but at first took it for a small, local storm which would pass well up ahead of us. However, the flashes gradually became more distinct and the wind slowly but steadily increased until the vessel was fairly flying. Finally, I became aware of a dark, black patch in the direction of the lightning flashes and decided it was time to call the captain.

While making my way down to the cabin I had a rather guilty feeling that I had let calling the skipper ride a bit too long. I poked my head into his room and called. Just then there was a roar from the deck, "BOSUN!"

I dashed out the forward companion and started aft, but was met by a yell.

"Call out all hands! Get those topsails in! Take in the outer and flying jibs and when you get done come back here and lower this spanker."

He paused just long enough to catch his breath, and as I streaked along the deck to get things going, he added, "Just what in hell did you think you were doing?"

We had three good able seamen out of four. This was all we needed to get the topsails clewed in in rapid order. They were left hanging when we got them to the mastheads. There was no time for tying them up; that small black patch I had seen now covered most of the sky to windward. The lightning was now punctuated by the rumble of thunder. The wind had hauled still farther forward and the vessel was diving into a choppy cross sea.

We hauled down the outer and flying jibs, then laid out on the plunging jibboom to make them fast. She was already thrusting her dolphin striker into the seas and it was wet work passing the gaskets —work we were anxious to get done in a hurry.

The full fury of the storm crashed down upon us as we reached the deck and started aft to take in the spanker. We got the great sail lowered without carrying anything away. We got it rolled up in the lazy jacks and made the boom secure with the sheet hauled flat, boom tackle secured, and crutch tackles in place. Then I was told a few things that any young officer need only be told once. Had the skipper not come on deck just when he did, the *Herbert L. Rawding* would certainly have been short of some sails, and the possiblity of more

During the gale of March 1941 a gull landed aboard the RAWDING. Here it rests on a hatch toward the end of the blow. The wind and seas have eased, but the decks show no signs of drying. This photograph shows clearly how the hatches were secured with tarpaulins, metal bars, and wooden hatch bars bolted down atop all (see photo, page 52). (Photo by author)

serious damage was not remote, for I had run the vessel, under full sail, smack into the face of a full-fledged gale out of the northwest.

It must have been well into our watch below before we left the deck to turn in. I was a chastened young man. I had put the ship in jeopardy, and caused extra work for all hands.

When I came on deck at 4:00 A.M., I found that the mate's watch had reefed down the fore, main, and mizzen, and the vessel was laboring heavily into a growing head sea. The wind had risen to full gale force and the vessel was shipping water forward in a dangerous manner. Few of the large four- or five-masted schooners could heave to comfortably in heavy weather. They would keep falling off the wind, roll terribly, and ship solid water forward. The *Rawding* was typical of this class of vessel. The only safe way to handle her, provided there was plenty of sea room, was to up helm, fall off, and

run before it. This is what Captain Decker decided on. We lowered the main and mizzen, swung off before the wind, and under reefed fore, staysail, and inner jib headed off southeasterly, where we had the whole ocean before us in which to run.

The wind increased still more that day. Several times we got too far off before the wind and the fore gaff jibed across with a tremendous CRASH! that shook the entire ship. We eventually lowered that foresail and the fore staysail. With only the jib we ran off under bare poles, before giant seas that raced after the vessel, towered over her stern as she sagged back into the trough from the last sea and then, with a mightly thrust, swept high in the air. The sea would roar by underneath and drop the struggling schooner into another great hollow, so the next monster could race down with terrifying force, to threaten and then sweep by in a furious rage at its inability to overwhelm the quarry. The wind moaned constantly in the rigging and occasional gusts would strike the vessel in a cloud of spray blown from the tops of the sea, laying the ship over from the force against her bare masts and shrieking through the taut wire stays.

For three days and three nights we ran before the gale. At times the fierce squalls would sweep down, blanketing sea and sky in a welter of flying rain and spray. Between the squalls the sun would shine brightly through racing clouds, or the stars would appear at night. The *Rawding* rode easily, with seas a point or so on the port quarter. Only occasionally would any amount of water come aboard, and then it was only the crests of seas slashing along the rails. One morning an exhausted sea gull landed on the after hatch and stayed there most of the morning. I photographed him before he recovered and took flight to battle the gale once more. Twice we got a little too directly before the

"African Sam" Wilson, the cook, was photographed aboard the five-masted schooner EDNA HOYT in 1935. He was cook aboard the RAWDING during both of the author's voyages.
(Photo by author)

following seas and the *Rawding*, unable to lift as quickly before the following seas, was pooped. Fortunately the yawl boat on the stern davits took most of the force of these boarding seas, and except for the helmsman and officer of the watch getting well soaked, there was no damage. I presume the vessel worked a bit, but the beauty of a steam donkey engine is the fact that the pumping is done by the chief. Unless he becomes worried, there is little need for anxiety on the part of the crew. Hand pumping would have been a different matter.

One morning as I came on deck Old Sam, the cook, was holding onto the spanker rigging and looking off to starboard.

"Look at dat, Mist Bowka," he remarked. About two miles away, a big tanker was slogging her way north and hitting those great seas, butt end on. As she drove her head into a sea her whole forward end would disappear in a smother of water, until little but the stack and after house were visible. She would clear herself and then dive again.

We stood there in silence for a couple of minutes. Sam finally shook his head and stated, "A've been in sailing vessels fo' sixty yeahs an' ain't nevah been in one of dem things. Ah ain't nevah goin' in one of dem. Dey's dangerous."

I thought about this wooden schooner with her aging iron fastenings and how easily she could spring a butt, fill up, and drown the lot of us. I looked at that old African who had left his native land as a young boy, had survived shipwreck, foundering, a fever-ridden barkentine from which he was one of three survivors, had been aboard a three-masted schooner that rode out the great "Portland Gale," and had his stomach ripped open by a drink-crazed wife who had been in an asylum for many years and whom he still loved. There was something solid and reassuring about Sam. He had told me much of his life story one storm-tossed evening when I reclined in an old Morris chair in the saloon and he braced himself in a chair chocked between the cabin table and the pantry. It had been too rough to sleep, but a fine time to yarn.

On the afternoon of the third day of this blow, the wind eased up and began backing to the southward. We hoisted our reefed fore, main, and mizzen and once again set a course to make up the 200-odd miles we had been blown off. It was slow going, as we were now heading into the same huge, rolling seas that had been driving us for three days. The old vessel rolled and plunged, but she kept her head in the right direction, at least for a while.

By sundown the breeze had dwindled to a gentle air, just enough to keep the sails full, and by midnight it had died entirely. The *Rawding* fell off into the trough of the swell and began to roll so violently that, once again, we were forced to lower all sail, this time in order to prevent them from slatting to pieces. There is nothing in the world like the thrashing of a large schooner rolling helplessly in the after swell of such a storm as we had been through. At the height of the storm the seas may have reached a height of from forty to fifty feet. By now they were down to about twenty feet, but to a vessel lying helplessly in the trough, such swells are of terrifying proportions. She rolled with monotonous regularity, putting first one rail and then the other into the water. Aloft, the topmasts swept a broad arc against the sky. Back and forth, back and forth the vessel rolled, as if she would snap the masts right out of her. It was difficult to stand on deck. It was almost impossible to stay in a bunk. In the galley and in the cabin pantry, doors flew open to shower pots and broken crockery about the decks. There was nothing to be done on deck. The rudder kicked so hard it was dangerous

to keep a man at the wheel. Kicking tackles were put on the tiller to control its thrashing and the wheel was lashed. Hour after hour the vessel rolled back and forth. I had the graveyard watch, from midnight to 4:00 A.M. I kept one man aft, near the wheel; the other stood lookout on the forecastle head. My only concern was to watch carefully in case something started to carry away.

The mate relieved me at 4:00 A.M. and I went below. I took off my boots and rolled into my bunk "all standing." With the vessel thrashing as she was, I wanted to be ready for the call, "ALL HANDS!" There was little comfort to be had under such circumstances. The cabin resounded with a variety of noises; the wash of water sweeping across the deck, the pounding of the rudder, the groaning of the ship's timbers, and the tramp of feet overhead as some piece of gear had to be made more secure. Nevertheless, I fell into a restless sleep, during which all sorts of wild dreams crossed my mind.

Still lying where it fell three days before, the mizzen topmast overhangs the RAWDING's port side. The seas have quieted and the schooner no longer rolls heavily, so it can now be brought aboard and lashed securely without risk of injury or further damage. (Photo by author)

Mate Berne Bradford went aloft to clear the rigging after the mizzen topmast carried away in the rolling seas following the March 1941 gale. Reefed sails have been set as a light breeze makes up. Because the vessel still rolls, full sails might slat heavily and have to be lowered again. (Photo by author)

When the call for breakfast came, I learned what all the commotion had been about. The mizzen port trestletree, which helped support the topmast, had carried away and the topmast, dropping straight down, had driven its butt into the corner of No. 2 hatch, laid over, and crashed through the port rail. It lay there with about twelve feet of its end projecting out over the side. The watch on deck lashed it down where it lay. When I came on deck, the mate was up on the masthead clearing the topmast rigging and lashing it clear of the gear for the mizzen sail. The vessel was still rolling twenty-five or thirty degrees and the sailors had not liked the idea of hanging on at the masthead to work, so the sixty-three-year-old mate went up himself. When I saw what had happened, I was a bit chagrined that I had not investigated the trouble more thoroughly when it happened. The captain asked me if I had heard the racket and I replied with a feeble excuse that I felt that if they had needed me they would have called. As bosun, I should have hit the deck without being called.

As the years have passed, I've taken time to look back on my many experiences in those old schooners. They were a school like no other could be. I learned that there were times when one could entirely forget himself and perform deeds that might win a medal in a military service, yet be considered routine in a sailing ship. I learned there were times when one could stand up and defy man or nature, and there were times when he must lay to, or even turn and run if he would survive. The main thing is to keep one's self-respect and earn the respect of those with whom you must exist.

We rolled in that calm for a couple of days, then a fair slant shoved us almost to Cape Lookout. Another nor'wester hit us off Cape Lookout, but it was nothing we couldn't handle under reefed lowers.

Suddenly I was awakened by a tremendous crash, followed by a couple of heavy thumps. I sprang from my bunk, threw on my boots and started for the deck, thinking that perhaps a sheet had carried away and that one of the booms with its heavy gaff and all the attached canvas had gone adrift and might be flailing across the deck. It was still dark when I paused at the top of the companionway and glanced forward from the coach house window. I could see forms up near the number two hatch, but there was no call for the watch. Sleepily deciding that not too much could have gone wrong, and there being no call for assistance, I decided the mate's watch felt they could handle the problem and went below again.

We took advantage of the Gulf Stream and made a course for Nantucket Shoals. A fresh nor'easter drove us back from Nantucket and brought real cold and our first taste of snow.

Willoughby Banks, the West Indian sailor who hated cold weather, stands watch in lee of forward house during the stormy passage of March 1941.
(Photo by author)

One of my fondest recollections of that trip is an event which occurred at this time. Our black crew were even less pleased at the prospect of cold weather than I was. I had the two best men in my watch. One was a man who had been in large schooners for years. The other was Joe, the Brava man. These two were as tough as they made them. In the other watch was our little Portugee, Manny, and the West Indian, Willoughby Banks.

Banks was a good sailor in ordinary weather, but the cold got him down. One night Old Joe had the wheel at the end of the watch. Joe scorned heavy clothing and would stand at the wheel with his shirt open at the neck, when I would be half frozen in an overcoat. When the mate came on deck to take over the watch, I gave him the course and he went off on some business of his own. Banks had not shown up to relieve Joe, so I stayed by the wheel, waiting for him to get the course before going below myself. After waiting about ten minutes, I became impatient and started forward to look for Banks.

As I reached the end of the house, I was startled by a huge, shapeless form that materialized out of the darkness. Suddenly the voice of Willoughby Banks spoke from the depths of the object and I knew it was no apparition. Back by the wheel, in the glow from the binnacle, this sight took some semblance of human form. Banks had put on every piece of clothing he owned, including his oilskins. Evidently deciding that even this would not keep him warm, he had stripped the blankets from his bunk and, with palm and needle, had sewn the blankets on. If I had been skipper, I think I would have been sorely tempted to wear ship or find a topsail that needed to be tied up, just to see how he would get around.

The nor'easter shoved us back in toward the

coast, and one cloudy morning, with the wind hauling from east to south and southwest, we made in past Block Island and into Vineyard Sound. With a fair wind and tide we swept up past Woods Hole and Vineyard Haven. The wind was still hauling and the glass was dropping. As we passed Woods Hole, Captain Decker looked hard at the signal tower by the lighthouse on Nobska Point.

"I've half a mind to anchor in Vineyard Haven. That glass don't look good to me." He paced the deck for a moment, then made up his mind. "Well, they don't have any storm warning flying, and they should have better information than I have." We continued on our way.

"I still don't like the looks of that glass," he remarked a bit later, but by that time it was too late to do much about it. We had swept past Vineyard Haven.

The light rain and the fresh southwesterly wind held as we put the wind astern off East Chop and shoved out by Cross Rip lightship. We had just jibed over and set a course for the Handkerchief Shoal lightship, and were straightening up the gear, when Captain Decker called out, "Get the topsails in fast! Haul down the headsails and stand by to anchor. All hands on deck!"

A quick glance to the northwest was enough to insure the most immediate compliance. A great dark line of cloud and snow was spreading out across the horizon. The rain, which had been with us all morning, had suddenly stopped. A puff of sharp, freezing air swept over the ship. The four topsails were quickly clewed in to the mastheads. There was not time to haul in sheets as the vessel was headed up into the wind, with sails slatting. Chain sheets and lignum vitae blocks slashed and thumped as the headsails were hauled down in the teeth of a furious onslaught of wind and hail. The mate leaned over the forecastle head, waiting for the vessel to lose headway, while one man stood by the compressor bar, to let the anchor drop at his signal. The skipper stood aft by the wheel, and I took charge of getting in sail.

Blinding snow struck us as the anchor was let go. We left the headsails trailing on the jibboom and hastened along the deck, slacking off boom tackles and hauling in sheets. Then we lowered the thrashing lower sails, starting with the fore and working aft. The schooner lay with her head to the wind and tide, riding to a full scope of chain on her port anchor. She jerked at the short, choppy seas, and spray flying across the decks froze as it landed. We tied up the topsails and headsails, then put reefs in all the lowers in case we had to pull out in a hurry.

Nantucket Shoals is one of the graveyards of the Atlantic Coast, and many a fine vessel, forced to anchor there to ride out such a gale, has gone to the bottom with no trace except drifting pieces of wreckage cast up on Nantucket or Monomoy Point. The six-masters *Ruth E. Merrill* and *Wyoming* were both lost in these waters in the winter of 1924. The *Wyoming* took all fourteen of her crew with her in a winter gale, including Captain Glaesel, who had been the *Rawding*'s master on her maiden voyage.

Reefing sail when freezing spray soaks your hands, making mittens almost useless and frozen rope and canvas so hard they have to be beaten with hand-spikes and belaying pins in order to be handled at all, is no picnic. At sea there is no such thing as quitting a job because it is too hard. When your life depends on the job you do, you do it in spite of almost impossible odds. Thus, we managed to get all four sails reefed, though we were soaked to the skin and half frozen inside, with ice flaking from our oilskins and boots. The deck was a mass of moving slush.

When the tide turned to the westward sometime in the afternoon, we were suddenly exposed to a new hazard. The strong current, sweeping in against the wind, swung the vessel broadside to the seas and at the same time chopped the seas into short, breaking waves that roared at the *Rawding* in such quick succession that she could not gather from one roll before another wave smashed at her side. The decks were constantly awash with slushy water, and ice formed on the sails and rigging until it would have been impossible to hoist sail had we desired. We let go the second anchor and rode to ninety fathoms of chain on each anchor, but in the shoal water (about six fathoms) the vessel reared and jerked like a wild creature in agony. We somehow hoisted the reefed spanker in an effort to keep her head to the wind, but this was only partially successful. Our only relief came when the tide turned to ebb. Then the vessel was both wind and tide rode and the seas felt more easy in their onward rush.

That night the officer of the watch spent most of his time in the donkey room, where it was necessary to keep an eye on the windlass. The *Rawding* was making heavy weather of it, in spite of the long scope of chain she had out. As every large sea struck her she would yank back with a rumble and such a crash that it seemed she would pull the windlass clear through the forward part of the ship. The chief stayed awake all night and kept steam in the boiler. From time to time, I let the man on anchor watch come in to warm up and took his place for a while.

The captain had been restless and worried all through the day, and when I went below at 8:00 P.M. he was in the donkey room. I turned in with

even my seaboots on. There was an empty, hollow feeling in the pit of my stomach, for I knew we were in one of the gravest situations I had experienced. I don't know if I took the time to think back on that night I had driven the *Rawding* into our big gale, a few weeks before. Captain Decker, against his own intuition, had run the vessel past a safe anchorage and must have been suffering similar pangs of guilt. His problem was worse than mine, for he had nobody to turn to for advice. The loneliness of command is absolute. When the ship strikes bottom and the master sees his men swept under by the raging sea, what torture must he undergo before a great sea washes him from his grasp on life and the green seas close over him forever.

At midnight, when the mate came to call me for the watch, he told me to come directly to the engine room. Here he informed me that the port anchor had carried away. He had given the starboard anchor its last 15 fathoms of chain. We were now riding to that anchor on 105 fathoms of chain, along with the weight of whatever was left of the port cable. He told me that he had not informed the skipper and that I was not to awaken him, because he needed whatever rest he could get as long as the starboard anchor held. I felt that this was the wrong thing to do, but the mate was my superior officer, a shipmaster in his own right, and I simply kept a doubly sharp watch. The way we were iced up, there was no possibility of making sail if we did drag or the other anchor carried away.

My watch passed without incident, and the mate took over again at 4:00 A.M. At breakfast the skipper asked me why he had not been called when the anchor let go. I told him it had not happened on my watch, and he let the matter drop.

There was no letup in the wind that day. We

had dragged a couple of miles toward Nantucket since anchoring, and the island was plainly visible astern. During the morning we hoisted the ensign upside down, as a signal of distress. Nothing came along until late afternoon when the collier *Hampden* came wallowing along in a smother of foam, as she bucked into the gale, en route to Hampton Roads. She noticed our signal and, after exchanging flag hoists and ascertaining our difficulty, called the Coast Guard to our assistance.

That night was almost a repetition of the one before. We spent it hoping the Coast Guard would get to us before the other anchor let go. However, it was not until the next morning that the cutter hove up alongside. It was too rough to think of getting a line aboard, except in the direst emergency, so the cutter anchored about a half mile away where she could keep an eye out for further trouble. It was

comforting to see that sleek, white craft rolling and pitching out there, with no other purpose than to see that no harm befell us. Still, we all knew that even the presence of the Coast Guard can not always prevent disaster. Through another night we stayed ready for any event. The wind still blew hard that night, but next morning the cutter sent over a ten-inch towing line, which we managed to get aboard.

The wind had eased up and the sun was warm enough to soften the ice which coated us. We beat the ice away with whatever was handy. It fell in chunks and sloshed around the decks. By noon we were able to set a couple of sails to steady the ship and give some assistance to the cutter. It was rather slow going, but we towed past the Stonehorse lightship and were out past Pollock Rip by dark. A big swell still rolled on and the towing was slow. I

The HERBERT L. RAWDING tows into Boston Harbor, 22 March 1941, at the end of her stormy passage north. Visible just forward of the mizzen shrouds is the hole in the rail made by the falling mizzen topmast. What looks like a hole in the vessel's side is a seagull in flight.
Photo by John L. Lochhead. (Courtesy Mariners' Museum of Newport News, Virginia)

In the RAWDING's hold, longshoremen swing the cargo
bucket into place, March 1941. They will then dig into the
"goatina" with shovels to fill the bucket. How many
shovelfuls are there in 1,600 tons? (Courtesy Giles M.S. Tod)

Boston Harbor, smelling a little high." At that
time the *Rawding* was not the last of the "four-
stickers," nor did she smell a little high. Goat
manure is not an objectionably odorous cargo.

It had been a rather ordinary, run-of-the-mill
passage of thirty days. It was just the same sort of
winter passage sailing vessels have had coming up
the coast since sailing vessels first started coming
up the coast. It was not exceptional for the troubles
we had. Except for the time on Nantucket Shoals,
it might possibly have been a passage forgotten
among a hundred others by some of the crew.

At the
Quincy Lumber
Company in
Quincy,
Massachusetts,
the author left
the schooner
THEOLINE
in August 1941,
after a voyage
as mate.
(Courtesy
Melvin Rand)

came on deck at midnight and discovered that the
towline was badly chafed. I put on more chafing
gear and slacked out the last possible bit of line.
However, off Highland Light, the line parted. More
sail was made and Captain Decker signaled with a
flashlight that we could proceed on our own.

The twenty-second of March 1941 was a
beautiful day. With a fresh southwesterly breeze,
we slid across Boston Bay. Before noon we had anchored on East Boston flats. When the port doctor
had cleared us, a newspaper reporter boarded.

On 23 March 1941 the *Boston Herald* reported
our trip: "Last 4-masted schooner in Harbor after
Long Trip." With typical inaccuracy, the paper
reported, "Ending a 30-day voyage up from Las
Piedras, Venezuela, the four-masted schooner
Herbert L. Rawding, last of the large four-stickers
left in commercial operation, arrived yesterday in

My Second Voyage in the *Herbert L. Rawding*, 1941-1942 · 5

At the end of every voyage a sailing vessel would pay off the entire crew. One man, usually the cook or mate, would be retained to look out for the vessel. If both were good men and a charter seemed likely as soon as cargo was out, both might be retained. The crew would quickly scatter and new faces would appear for another voyage.

Mr. Bradford had had enough of schoonering and headed home. I planned to return for another voyage, but headed for Vermont to visit my mother and wait for a call. About a week after arriving home, I received a phone call asking me to ship as mate in the four-master *Theoline*. She had lain in Jonesport, Maine, over the winter and had been sold to new owners, the last of a fleet of schooners owned by B.F. & C.F. Small of Machias, Maine.

I decided it was better to sail as mate and get some time for sitting for a master's license than to make another trip as bosun, which would not help me in that regard. The vessel was to go to a shipyard in Nova Scotia for drydocking and necessary repairs. This meant that I would acquire considerable time before we arrived back in Boston with a cargo of lumber. I made that voyage and paid off in Quincy, Massachusetts.

Meanwhile, the war in Europe had escalated, the British had been driven out of France, German U-boats were sinking allied ships at an alarming rate, and freights for neutral ships were heading for the sky.

While I was sailing as mate of the *Theoline*, the *Rawding* was not idle. Before she left Boston, my friend Bob Robinson rejoined her as mate. On 12 April she sailed from Boston for Norfolk and arrived 21 April. Here, she loaded coal for Galion Bay, Martinique, and sailed on 2 May.

Galion Bay, on the windward side of Martinique, is a very uneasy anchorage for a sailing vessel, but the cargo was discharged in good time and the *Rawding* set sail for Turk's Island prior to 12 June. At Turk's Island a cargo of salt was loaded for Yarmouth, Nova Scotia, and delivered there 24 July 1941.

From Yarmouth, the vessel sailed to Sheet Harbor, Nova Scotia, to load lumber for New York. Bob told me he cautioned Captain Decker about the vessel's crankiness with a deckload, but a full cargo was stowed aboard. Again, she lay down on her side in any sort of a breeze, but better winds favored her than thay had in 1937; she sailed from

A Royal Canadian Air Force pilot photographed the RAWDING from above as she approached Yarmouth, Nova Scotia, in 1941. She is hard on the wind, making plenty of leeway as she stems the tide.
Photo by John Green. (Courtesy Yarmouth Historical Museum)

The new foremast installed at Perth Amboy was not of the finest quality. It had come from a much larger vessel and had been used as a wharf camel at Portland for some years. It was towed down from Portland and turned to size on the Perth Amboy Drydock Company spar lathe. When the mast was brought out to the wharf, the old mast hoops were first slid on. The trestletrees, crosstrees, and all the ironwork were reuseable and, with some chopping and planing, the bands were driven into place. The rigging had been overhauled and was slid back into position with care to be sure that all was replaced exactly as it had come off the old mast. Otherwise, the shrouds would come down in uneven lengths. The workers at Perth Amboy were old hands at repairing and rigging large wooden sailing vessels.
(Courtesy G.I. Johnson)

Sheet Harbor on 28 August, arrived in New York 18 September, and was towed to Newtown Creek, Brooklyn, to discharge. Bob had rigged an inclinometer in his room and told me she often lay down over thirty degrees with no topsails set. It was an unpleasant passage.

Once the lumber was out, the vessel towed to Perth Amboy, New Jersey, to be hauled out. The foremast was showing signs of rot about the masthead, and a big spar, that had been in the water for many years, was towed down from Portland. The old mast was unstepped, and the Perth Amboy Drydock Company had a lathe that easily turned out a new one, twenty-seven inches in diameter and ninety-eight feet in length.

It was while the ship was at Perth Amboy that I took my gear aboard and shipped in my old position as bosun aboard the *Rawding*. It was good to be back with my friend Bob, and I turned to with a will.

This view of the RAWDING at Perth Amboy in the fall of 1941 was undoubtedly taken from the rigging of the four-master JAMES E. NEWSOM on the floating drydock at Perth Amboy Drydock. The author stands on the martingale backrope, tending the yawlboat painter. The old foremast lies on the pier.
(Courtesy G.I. Johnson)

Looking forward along the deck of the HERBERT L. RAWDING at Perth Amboy Drydock Company, 1941. The foremast is still missing; the old topmast lies on deck. It was later the author's task to get this topmast sawn up for firewood. Both the mate and bosun performed many manual chores when no other crew was aboard. Hatch covers are removed to allow ventilation of the hold. The three large hatches allowed cargo to be stowed evenly without too much trimming. When loading coal the vessel could be shifted so any one of the three hatches would be under the chute. The RAWDING had two decks, the between deck having about seven feet of headroom under the deck beams. Under the partly opened hatch covers can be seen the strongbacks. A very heavy one in the center of the hatch supported the inboard edge of each hatch cover. A lighter strongback held up the center of each cover. When the covers were on, three layers of tarpaulin were drawn across. Metal battens on the sides of the hatch were removed, the edge of the tarpaulin punched to fit over the bolts, and the iron battens put on with nuts and washers to secure all. The big wooden hatch bars were laid fore-and-aft across the hatch, one on either side. One of the bolts over which these were slipped is visible hanging down on the after side of the hatch coaming. The bolt would be held erect and the hole on the end of the hatch bar slipped over and bolted down (see photo, page 40). Many times, hundreds of tons of water swept at will across these decks, and a stove-in hatch would mean sudden death.

(Courtesy G.I. Johnson)

Looking aft along the deck of the RAWDING at Perth Amboy Drydock Company, 1941. Even in the shipyard, the mate has made sure certain lines have been coiled in somewhat shipshape manner. The foresail has been rolled up and is stowed under the tarpaulin between the crew's water tank and the main hatch. Note that the white paint has become dingy and the slush (grease) on the masts has turned very dark during the vessel's stay in port. The masts will be scraped and new slush applied in the next port where coal, with its attendant dust, is not being loaded or discharged. Slush was necessary to preserve the masts from both chafing by the hoops of the sails and the ravages of weather. The lower ends of the RAWDING's shrouds are spliced, rather than turned up and seized around a heart, which was more common.

Splicing was neater and would last longer, if the wire was served the entire length and tar was applied once a year to keep all waterproof. At the forward end of the cabin, on the port side, is a big box, which on a smaller vessel would cover an engine for the bilge pumps. On the RAWDING this was a locker for the bosun's stores, as pumping was done by steam, under the donkeyman's jurisdiction, from the forward house. At the corner of the cabin is a rainwater barrel.
(Courtesy G.I. Johnson)

Riggers at Perth Amboy Drydock Company bend on the RAWDING's jib, 1941. Even in older days shore riggers were considered sloppy in their work. One of the first tasks the mate would undertake when a crew came aboard was to put the rigging in seamanlike order. The photographer snapped this scene from the wharf after the author mentioned to him that few photographs showed sailors doing their routine work.
(Courtesy G.I. Johnson)

The mate (right) and a sailor put a proper harbor furl in the jib. The massive headgear on a large schooner is illustrated by the RAWDING's bowsprit, which was forty-six feet long and twenty-six inches in diameter. Because of rot under the cap, a new end was scarfed on, and the joint was secured with the three iron bands visible between the inner bobstay band, left, and the mate at right. With the new foremast stepped and the headstays rigged, the hanks of the jib have been bent on and the jackline at the tack has been laced. The jib foot is secured to a club, which slides back and forth for several feet on a sliding gunter. When the sail is set the club slides aft, and the jackline holds the jib tack to the stay. When the sail is lowered the club slides forward, letting the hanks slide down the stay as near the jibboom as possible.
(Courtesy G.I. Johnson)

There was plenty of activity at the Perth Amboy drydock. Besides the *Rawding*, two other four-masters were present. The Nova Scotia-owned *James E. Newsom* was hauled out, and the schooner *Brina Pendleton* was being converted to a barge by Captain Will Plummer, formerly master of my schooner, *Helen Barnet Gring*, and Captain Will Davis, a man who had been master of schooners all the way from two to six masts.

When the new mast was stepped and rigged, we shipped a crew sent over from South Street by ''Nigger'' Charlie Hoyt. This time our crew were white and two were former shipmates. Eddie Moran was a young Irish fellow from East Boston. The other three were Scandinavians, old timers, and fine seamen when they sobered up. Sore Eye Martin and I had been shipmates in two other vessels. The other two were both named Pete. It was a fine crew, and we towed out one morning, set sail, and made our way to Newport News, where we arrived 14 November. We loaded 1,660 tons of gas coal for Fort-de-France on 16 November.

A diary was a thing that I always wrote by fits and starts. Some voyages were never recorded, and

others only partially. On Thursday, 20 November, 1941, I resumed writing:

> Day being 'Roosevelt's Thanksgiving' gave the boys a holiday in the forenoon. The vessel loaded Friday at Pier 16 and has been waiting for a chance since then. Have 1660 tons of gas coal aboard. After dinner there was a moderate S.W. breeze so started to get under way. Wind became light and dark clouds came up from the westward so we anchored in Hampton Roads; the captain fearing it would back around to N.E. during the night. Day ends partly cloudy with moderate S.W. wind.

I should mention that old African Sam was again our cook and Mrs. Decker had joined her husband for the voyage. I presume we may have had a pot roast for ''Roosevelt's Thanksgiving'' as Captain Decker was not one to splurge on turkey and all the fixings, even though freights were higher than they had been in years, and Captain Rickson was not around to buy turkey.

> Fri. Nov. 21st. Day begins cloudy with mod. N.E. wind. During the morning we bunkered up the chief. In the afternoon bent on our new fore topsail. During the day there were a great many airplanes around and many of them were torpedo carriers, each with a yellow nosed torpedo stuck under it.
>
> There are a great many Navy ships around, including a large airplane carrier. We believe it is the *Illustrious*.

Monday, 24 November, began with a strong north-northeast wind and rain squalls, and we had to tie up the headsails and topsails, which had been left hanging in anticipation of getting underway again. Clad in oilskins and boots, we made our way out onto the jibboom to secure the outer and flying jibs, then the four sailors, one to a mast, clambered aloft to secure the topsails.

By mid-afternoon the sky was clearing and,

On a beautiful fall day at Perth Amboy, the RAWDING is almost ready for sea. The new foremast has been stepped, and a man is aloft seizing on the electric forward riding light. The foresail and foretopsail still have to be bent, and the halyards need to be set up a bit. Soon the provisions and crew will be put aboard and a tug will take her to sea. (Courtesy G.I. Johnson)

with the wind northerly, we got sail on again and passed out by Cape Henry on a voyage that would prove eventful. Captain Decker had brought Mrs. Decker along for the voyage, and we looked forward to a pleasant winter in the West Indies. I always enjoyed it when captains had their wives aboard, because the crew kept cleaner, language, especially back aft, was better, and most of these women stayed in their place without interfering with the crew.

We started off in great style. The bottom was clean, and most of the old sails that had plagued Captain Torrey had been replaced. The second night out a steamer tried to cross our bow, but we were making about nine knots. Instead of bearing away to go under our stern, he came up and up until we were on a parallel course, and it was quite a while before he could work far enough ahead to bear away on his course. I had the watch and enjoyed the sport. It was always fun to give a steamer a run for his money.

As soon as we got offshore the soogee buckets were brought out and we started to wash a couple of months' accumulated dirt off the paint. I made a notation in my journal: "Paint washing not going too well. That Newtown Creek stain is hard to get off — Have to use ashes along with the soda and then the dirt comes off hard. This is the worst I ever saw. Well the weather is fine and bids to stay so for a while."

Later, "This is the sort of weather men go to sea for. The moon is just past the first quarter and lights up the sea beautifully. The weather is mild and the breeze steady. We are going along without lights in order to save our batteries, which are old and should have been replaced for this trip. Some economy, what with prices going up all the time . . . ."

Poor old Sam was having a tough time with his rheumatism and was upset that Mrs. Decker tried to help him. His meals were usually late, and often the watch were late coming on deck. In a vessel where one works a twelve-hour day, four on and four off, those few minutes extra on deck are a source of annoyance, but Sam was not a man one could get angry with. We bore a hand where we could and felt sorry for him.

On this voyage I often thought of the words chief Bean had given me a year before, on the occasion when Captain Torrey and Bob were fired and Captain Decker took over. I knew Bean had sailed with Decker.

"Well, he's a damn good seaman," replied the old fellow, "but I'll tell you one thing, he hates mates."

With a tug on her starboard quarter, the HERBERT L. RAWDING tows out from Perth Amboy Drydock, November 1941, bound for Newport News and Martinique. The American flag is painted on her side as a sign of neutrality, though soon all such pretense would come to an end. The bottom was clean, but the topsides were only partially painted as that task was planned for the crew while the coal was offloaded at Martinique. (Courtesy G.I. Johnson)

Bob and I considered ourselves competent schoonermen, took pride in our work, knew the ship and her gear, and had a good crew of veteran sailors. Bob had made his first voyage aboard a schooner with Decker in the four-master *Edward L. Swan*, and had served in the *Rawding* the previous voyage. I don't know what got into the man this trip. One day he would be quite pleasant, and the next would complain about everything we did. He would stand by the wheel and talk with the helmsman, but maintain a stony silence with the officer of the watch.

Of course, Bob and I began to grouse about the food. It wasn't all Sam's fault, because the skipper went on an economy kick. Freights were rising, and we could see no reason why there shouldn't be a better variety of chow. Aside from that, the bosun's locker was sparsely supplied with new rope and other supplies. Of course the owners expected to make a profit and didn't want it all eaten up in ship's expenses. We could make do.

There was plenty of wind but mostly ahead. We were deeply laden and, with the sheets hardened in, we shipped plenty of water across the decks. We wanted to pass to the northward of Bermuda, make enough easting to work through the horse latitudes and be able to reach down outside the islands, round Martinique, and come up under the lee of the island. If one gets too far to leeward, it can be long, hard work beating up against the northeast trades and a westerly setting current. This was a road Captain Decker knew well. I now regret not having written down our daily positions, but bosuns are not much concerned with navigation.

The wind eased up, but the big swell kept rolling. At times we could make headway, then fall off into the trough, where the sails would slat for a while, until another breeze filled them. This was hard on the gear, and we were continually lowering one sail or another to replace stitching in the seams.

On 1 December we had rain squalls and filled all our barrels and tanks. With the first shower we would break out brooms and sweep off the tops of the cabin and forward house. There were scuppers with canvas hoses hung from the forward corners of the cabin trunk and from the after end of the forward house. Beneath these were old beef barrels, which quickly filled. With wooden buckets, which had originally been salt mackerel kits, we filled the engine room tanks, the galley tank, the crew's wash water tank, and the tank for the captain's bathroom. Every bucket was filled, and it was the opportunity for a good bath and clothes washing spree. When the sun came out the decks would be festooned with laundry drying in the warm sun.

Meanwhile, we weren't making much time on our way to Martinique, and Captain Decker's humor spread to the rest of us. I'll quote from my journal again.

This 'Old Man' is a menace to organized work around here. He can't make up his mind what he wants to do half the time. All of a sudden, this afternoon, he decided he wanted to put sail on her and began hollering. We got the flying jib without him bothering, then started to get the spanker ready. We were just about to begin hoisting when we discovered he was wearing the ship around and the sails were about to come over. Got that squared away, and shifted the spanker boom across and he decided he wanted to hoist the spanker topsail clear of the masthead, so we led the halliard to the winch. Then he decided to let that go and hoist the spanker anyhow. It's almost as bad as the old *Edward R. Smith*, with Captain Baird. Bob is disgusted, Sam and the chief ditto and so am I. But, cheer up boys, the trip has hardly yet begun. 8:00 P.M. Fair with moderate S.E. wind. Vessel headed up about E.N.E. The 'old man' stayed on deck and never spoke a word.

So it went. Light winds, mostly from the eastward, until December seventh. Things went peacefully during the morning, and we got a little fair wind to set her on course during the afternoon.

I had the eight to twelve watch. About nine o'clock the captain came on deck.

"Well, Bosun," he remarked, "it's a good thing you're not at home. You'd be in the army or navy tomorrow."

I'd heard so much of his gloomy talk that I didn't bother to answer.

"The Japanese have bombed the Philippines and Pearl Harbor and sunk our entire navy!" he proclaimed.

I wasn't about to hoist in such nonsense. Perhaps the Japanese had done some bombing, but I wasn't about to believe they had sunk our entire navy. I gave him so little satisfaction that he finally stumped below. As the watch dragged on I began to wonder just what had happened, and when I called Bob at one bell (quarter to twelve) decided I'd get an honest answer. Bob had his personal radio in his room.

Going down into the cabin, I opened Bob's door.

"One bell," I called.

"OK," I got the usual answer. "How's the weather?"

"Weather's alright, but turn on your radio. When you come on deck tell me if it's true."

I was waiting by the coach house door when Bob came on deck. "It's all true," he said, and filled me in on the details.

Life for us went on as usual, but now we knew it would soon change.

On 8 December I noted:

Fair with fresh N.E. wind, course E.S.E. Tore the mizzen topsail, setting it this morning, so are going to send it down and bend our new one. All other sail set. I wish I were home now, so I could get started with the rest of the gang in whatever service I am to be in. Well, here I am and the trip has only started, so I guess it will be some time yet before I get into the fight. Nobody aboard is at all excited, or even surprised, except we really hadn't expected the Japanese to drag us into the war in such dramatic fashion.

The wind fell light, but the pesky swell continued. At times we would take in all sail to prevent them from slatting to pieces. If a breeze sprang up and showed signs of freshening, we would make sail again. All too often it would die out after a while and down would come the sails again.

On the eleventh, a couple of military planes swooped around and looked us over. We thought that was just fine. The weather remained about the same, and we began to wonder what was going on when these navy planes took to visiting us in pairs, both morning and afternoon. They were two-seater planes, and the after cockpits had machine gunners who trained their barrels on us as they zoomed by. We decided they were training craft.

The night of 14 December was again calm. We lowered sail once again and rolled. With daylight on the fourteenth a modest easterly wind sprang up, and we made all sail again after breakfast.

Suddenly the air swarmed with airplanes, and smoke appeared on the horizon. Soon a large aircraft carrier, with a cruiser and two destroyers, bore down on us, but passed a couple of miles ahead. One destroyer, the U.S.S. *Stack*, broke away from the group, swept down alongside, stopped, lowered a launch filled with men and charged off again.

Half a dozen machine guns were pointed at us as the boat came alongside, and a horde of sailors swarmed aboard with guns at the ready. Two officers hopped aboard and made their way aft, to where Captain and Mrs. Decker awaited them. Soon they disappeared below, to look over our papers. I presume our crew looked as ugly as captured Germans, and there was no communication between our crew and our captors.

Soon the captain walked forward with the two officers and told me to take off a hatch cover. The mate suggested that they couldn't see anything anyhow and it would be easier for them to take a couple of flashlights and go down through the grating in the engine room. To this they agreed.

Gas coal is about as dusty a product as one could wish. After a while, two much begrimed naval officers emerged from the hold, looked each other over, and began to laugh. One of the officers remarked that he thought he'd sue the United States Government. By this time the tension was relieved and the guns pointed at the deck instead of at us. It wouldn't have mattered what we had hidden under that coal, they never could have found it without towing us to port and discharging us.

It seems that the first planes that found us reported they had sighted a ship just sitting in one place and making no headway. This sounded suspicious, and as successive reports came in that sometimes the ship had sail set and sometimes lay there under bare poles, they began to wonder if we might be a supply ship for German submarines, a spy ship, or have some other hostile mission. Why would a vessel just lie there and not go much of anywhere? On top of all that, it may be that we lay right on the proposed track the carrier intended to

The yawlboat seen from the deck. We hoped we would not need this on our passage from Cap-Haitien to Baltimore, through submarine infested waters in 1942. Note lack of sail or oars. (Courtesy M.G. Robinson)

use. It doesn't seem reasonable that such an armada set out to investigate a lone schooner becalmed on an empty ocean.

One of our inspecting officers told us there had been some trouble at Martinique, but suggested we proceed.

Eventually we worked our way into the trade winds and picked up Sombrero Light on the evening of 23 December. With the vessel close hauled on the wind, we sailed down with Saba Island to leeward.

By this time everybody, including Mrs.

Decker, was trying to catch a fish to relieve the monotonous diet of salt horse(beef), hash, and stew. Sam did his best, but didn't have much to work with. There were dolphin and bonito playing around the ship. We skipped rags with hooks over the bows, and there was another trailing from the taffrail, but nary a fish could we entice aboard.

We clipped along to leeward of St. Eustatius and St. Kitts on the twenty-third, and Montserrat was abeam late on the twenty-fourth. That day I went down to the lazarette and brought up a Christmas box my mother had sent me. Mrs. Decker had been on tenterhooks since this box arrived, prior to our sailing. She kept asking if I'd peeked into it, but I told her that would spoil the fun.

On Christmas Day we had passed Gaudeloupe and were near Dominica at noon. It was then that I opened the box. I had to do this with Mrs. Decker present, and she was more excited than I. There was a pair of woolen gloves, eight pairs of socks, a necktie, a book, *Pattern of Conquest* by Joseph Harsch, two boxes of candy, and a small Dutch cheese. I shared the eatables with the others and thought what a mother I had, to think of sending such a welcome gift.

We made the north end of Martinique at daybreak of 28 December and, after beating up all day, anchored in the harbor of Fort-de-France about 6:30 P.M. The authorities came aboard immediately and left a naval officer to keep an eye on us. He was given the spare room in the cabin and was with us throughout our stay in port. Unfortunately, none of us could speak French, and he spoke no English. We could get no information about the political situation from him.

As usual, my diary was neglected in port. The Yankee dollar went a long way. Bob and I would often skip supper and repair to a bistro where, for a few francs, we could purchase a bottle of rum, which came with a lime and a bottle of cane syrup. After a couple of drinks we would wander off to the dining room. Langoustea, the southern version of a lobster, would be on the menu. The rub was that one could only purchase half a langoustea on a single night. One evening they would serve the tails, the next night you had to eat the forward end. We didn't care. It was better than Sam's hash and lobscouse. After dinner there were places where the girls were willing, and we would roll back to the wharf in the late hours, find a boatman, and return to the ship.

Meanwhile, we had readied the ship for discharging. The hatch covers were taken off, sail covers put on, the booms hoisted clear of the activity, and falls rove for the chief. Lighters were brought alongside, with a gang of black stevedores carrying shovels. We carried a big bucket which they filled with coal. The chief then hoisted it over the side and it was dumped into the lighters. It was a dusty job in the tropical heat. We tried to find work to keep our crew occupied, but it was difficult with coal dust over everything.

Captain Decker decided we could paint the sides of the ship and told me to cover over the American flags we had painted on the sides as a sign of neutrality. Now that we were at war, he felt there was no longer a need for these. As I saw the flag being painted over on the port side my anger rose and I approached the skipper.

"Captain," I said, "I'd like to keep that flag on the starboard side. Any submarine we see is going to know what we are, and we can't get out of their way. If they're going to sink her, let her go down with her colors." That was one time Captain Decker entirely agreed. We sailed with that flag proudly proclaiming our nationality.

It was strange to be in a port where we didn't know whether we were considered friend or foe. The French West Indies were committed to the Vichy government. Since we had brought a valuable cargo, the officials were friendly, but we never felt entirely at ease when ashore. One night there was a big celebration in the city. I believe it was Marshall Petain's birthday. There were fireworks and big celebrations, but our crew did not go ashore.

It took until 17 January 1942 to discharge all the coal. It was out at 3:00 P.M., and we got underway at 5:00 P.M. for Cap-Haitien, Haiti. There we would load logwood for Baltimore.

With empty hold, the *Rawding* was her usual cranky self. We sailed down to leeward of the islands under three lowers and a couple of head sails most of the way. We heard that German submarines had sunk a few steamships up on the coast and gave some passing thought to our own inability to avoid the same fate if we, too, should meet a submarine.

Anchor was dropped at Cap-Haitien on 25 January. We soon had the ship ready to take on cargo. Staging was put over the side and the pieces of wood passed, one at a time, up the staging, tossed down the hatch, and stowed by men below. It is heavy stuff, dark red in color, is crooked, and has hollows that hide such interesting creatures as scorpions, centipedes, small snakes, and spiders. When rain fell, the water would gather in some of the hollow spots and turn a beautiful wine red. In spite of all this, it was much used in the manufacture of rich blue and purple dyes. The longshoremen would come out at six in the morning and work until six at night. I was told that for this labor they were paid the equivalent of fifty cents a day

News of sinkings along the coast came in

A Perth Amboy rigger sets up the rigging on the fore topmast as part of the contract. As soon as a crew comes aboard, they will go aloft to do a more seamanlike job than a yard rigger is likely to leave. After all, he won't be aboard to worry about it when the going is rough.
(Courtesy G.I. Johnson)

every day. The captain tried to persuade Mrs. Decker to fly home, but she would have none of it. She would stay in the ship. The ship's agents were fine, friendly people and Mrs. Decker spent some time at their home.

Poverty has always been a way of life in Haiti, and an American dollar could be stretched a long way. One morning a man approached the ship in an old boat. "Buy langoustea?" he called.

"How much?" I inquired.

"Fifty cent," he waved his hand over the whole lot in the bottom of the boat. I called to the chief and asked if he'd like to buy some lobster and split the cost. He agreed and the fisherman put about twenty of the things into a basket while I dropped down a line.

"You got tin can?" he asked. "Big can." He waved his arms to indicate a five-gallon tin, such as we got linseed oil in. Yes, I had such a can. We had just finished scraping the topmasts and I had such a can.

"No money. You give can." It seemed we were both quite happy with our bargain.

One thing a visitor to Haiti never forgets is the sound of drums. Soon after the sun goes down the distant booming begins and goes on into the wee hours of the morning. It came from the city and it came from the hills and there was mystery in the sound. A little black fellow came aboard and asked if we'd like to have him arrange a voodoo session, but we had little interest in such a party. He had more luck with poor old Sam, whose legs were swollen so badly with his rheumatism that he could hardly stagger back from the galley to the cabin with meals for the officers. Bob and I had taken to carrying his basket for him.

Sam hired a witch doctor, who came out to mutter incantations and administer mysterious potions. He imagined that these ministrations gave some relief, but was seldom free of pain. Sixty years in sailing vessels is a long time. I'm certain Sam never again went to sea.

When the hold was full, we hoped the captain would call it enough, in view of our knowledge of the crankiness of the ship. However, the captain let them load it up to about the top of our rails. This would make her tender, but she could probably carry it. If things got too bad, we could probably heave it over the side.

Two other four-masters were also in our area. Our old friend, the *Anna R. Heidritter*, was loading logwood at Port-au-Prince. The *Albert F. Paul* was loading salt at Turk's Island. Though we might never sight them, we would have company on the way north.

We made our way over to Crooked Island Passage and worked up by San Salvador. The war news was getting worse, and sinkings along the coast were reported daily.

Captain Decker suddenly decided that such energy as was left in our batteries would be used for sidelights. On the trip south he wouldn't let us use them. Now, with ships being sunk all around us, he decided we should have them. Bob finally persuaded him to let us make canvas covers to cap them. We rigged trip lines that could pull the caps off if we sighted another ship. Bob and I were convinced that all other ships would be sailing without lights. We were right.

While at Cap-Haitien, Bob had decided to check out our yawl boat, the motorboat that hung on davits over the stern. This boat had remained hung over the stern for a couple of years, with a canvas cover over it, and was little used. He discovered that the stern was badly dry-rotted. He next got permission to bring the dory forward on the deckload and rig two falls so it could be hoisted over the side in an instant.

When the ship left Haiti, the captain purchased several chickens and a turkey. I believe the chickens cost about twenty cents each, and the turkey fifty cents. One Sunday morning Sam approached me and asked if I would hold the turkey while he cut its head off.

"Why don't you get one of the sailors?" I asked.

"None of dem sailors will do it," Sam replied. "Dey too chicken hearted. Ah tell dem day don't deserve no turkey. Dey don't mind goin' ashore, get drunk an' maybe kill a man in a fight, but dey won't even hep me kill dat turkey fo dey own din-

ner." We had the bird for dinner. I'd lived too long on a farm to be squeamish.

Twice we made in on the coast and were twice blown off. One afternoon I had the watch while we were coming back on the coast. I looked to the westward and saw two great plumes of black, oily smoke rising heavenward. I called the captain, who stomped up the steps, took the glasses from me, and looked long and hard.

"That's just those turpentine burners on the Carolina coast," he remarked, gave the glasses back, and went below. I knew they were ships afire, but also knew it was useless to argue.

A few nights later, we were lazing around in a

This view of the RAWDING's stern shows clearly the spanker boom tackles and yawl boat stowage. At the end of the boom, a seagull perches on the reef tackle block, used to haul out the reef band when shortening sail. With the sail furled, the boom is supported by the topping lifts, one on each side. The large triple block below the boom is the sheet block. Just forward of that the crotch tackles have been set up to immobilize the boom. They might also be used to haul it aweather when tacking. The block beneath the boom with the falls leading forward is the boom tackle, used to help control the boom while sailing. In a calm, with the vessel rolling, it is used to keep the boom from swinging wildly from side to side. With the wind aft and the boom out, it is led forward to prevent a jibe. In a controlled jibe, it is used to ease the boom over. The yawl boat rests on two strongbacks shoved out over the rail cap and lashed to U-bolts on the inboard side. The boat is lashed securely to the rail with canvas gripes.
(Courtesy G.I. Johnson)

fog, somewhere south of Cape Hatteras. There was just enough swell to give the booms an occasional lift, enough to make a block creak or thump. During my watch I heard sort of a "thrum, thrum, thrum." It was a sound I remembered hearing off New London when a submarine passed us one calm day in those waters. If it were a ship, I reasoned, it would keep moving along and soon be out of hearing. Once again I called the captain.

He came on deck, listened a while, and said, "Just one of those Norwegian motor ships." With that he stomped below. The mate heard it for some time during his watch, and we were certain it was a submarine on the surface charging its batteries. If we'd had an engine he would have heard us, but a silent sailing ship was not picked up on his listening device.

The next morning we picked up a light southwest breeze, but visibility remained poor. I had the forenoon watch, and Captain Decker paced the quarterdeck, binoculars in hand. He was looking and listening for Diamond Shoals lightship. Eventually I had the temerity to suggest that, in view of the many ships that were being sunk, the lightship might have been removed. With a glare, he passed the glasses to me and stomped below.

Visibility was about a mile, and I began scanning the waters carefully. Finally, something became visible on the port bow; it looked like a big triangle sitting on the water. Calling the captain, I passed the glasses to him. After scanning the object for a couple of minutes, while we gradually drew closer, he passed the glasses to me and without a word went below. The object was a torpedoed ship that had rolled over as it sank. Part of the bow and bottom remained above the water. I now knew that Captain Decker realized there was a war on.

All that day our gentle breeze wafted us along.

When night came, we could see the lights of the shore. The next morning we could see all sorts of navy and other craft going in and out by Cape Henry. We signaled for a pilot, but nobody paid us the slightest attention. Noon was approaching, we had a fair wind, there was a couple of miles visibility, and Captain Decker came to a conclusion. "Well, I don't really need a pilot. I've come in here many a time without one."

It wasn't long before we saw the misty shape of a steamship ahead. We were making for it when the pilot boat came tearing up at full speed, blinker flashing and horn tooting. Suddenly, we could hear them through a megaphone.

"GET OUT OF THERE! YOU'RE IN A MINEFIELD!"

"Can you tow us out?" asked the captain.

"I won't come in there. If you can get out, I'll put a pilot aboard."

"Haul down your headsails," screamed the skipper. He threw the wheel over.

"Drop the anchor!" he cried as the vessel came to the wind. In a moment the anchor flew from the hawsepipe and we lay back on the chain.

By the time we anchored, we had gone in beyond speaking range of the pilot boat. It was now evident to everybody that we could be blown sky high at any moment, by just swinging too far in any direction. From then on there was no panic. Captain Decker assessed the two courses we could make good if we hove up the anchor. The wind was somewhat off the land, and our best chance was to break away on the starboard tack, which would head us offshore. This was the way we worked it. The anchor was hove short, and the foresail was slacked off and held to starboard by the fore boom tackle. The spanker was hove off to port by the crutch tackle. As the anchor broke clear, the

Relaxing on the forward hatch, one of the crew reads the paper. With her new foremast in and foresail bent on and hanging in lazy jacks, the RAWDING is nearly ready for sea. The after side of the forward house has three doorways. The one at left leads into the galley. At right are a single and a double door into the engine room. The drum for the hoisting tackle is just inside the double door, where the engineer's controls are. At sea a low presssure of steam was always kept in the boiler. Though he stood no regular watch, the "chief" was always on call. He had a windowless room between the galley and engine room.
(Courtesy G.I. Johnson)

staysail and jib were hoisted, held to starboard by their tail ropes, and the vessel's head swung to port and offshore.

As the ship's head swung away, the headsails and foresail were let over. All sails filled on the starboard tack, and we stood away for the pilot boat, which waited patiently. They dropped a yawl over the side, and a young pilot scrambled up our side on a ladder we hung over.

Captain Decker had told the pilot boat that we were a bit short of food, and they sent over a few fresh vegetables and, best of all, some coffee. I don't know why we should have been short of anything. We were thirty days out of Cap-Haitien, where food was cheap. Thirty days was not exces-

sive for that time of year, and freights were high enough so the ship could afford to store up. Nobody had really gone hungry, but being out of coffee was a foul blow.

We thought our troubles were over, once the pilot was aboard, but the wind died out and the current set us backward, down the shore. All night we drifted. In the morning we picked up another light breeze. Our pilot had never brought a sailing vessel in and was nervous. About noon, the pilot boat bore down to see how we were making out, and our pilot asked if his captain would come aboard to bring us through the minefield. This he agreed to do, guided us well into the Chesapeake, and returned to the pilot boat.

We still didn't get much assistance from the wind and were five more days working our way to Baltimore. Captain Decker finally relaxed, and the pilot was having a wonderful time. It was months since he'd made a trip as easy. Our thrifty captain had nothing to complain about. The pilot had brought fresh food and coffee. The charge was the same if it took one day or ten. We were clear of submarines and would soon be home.

On 23 March we arrived in Baltimore and were towed to the pier of J.S. Young and Company, to deliver the last cargo of logwood ever to arrive by sailing vessel. We had been thirty-six days on passage and, besides weathering a couple of gales, had worked our way through seas where submarines were sinking ships at will. The bad weather and poor visibility had proved our salvation. The *Anna R. Heidritter* was wrecked, and the *Albert F. Paul* was sunk by a submarine. Nothing was ever heard of her crew.

As we towed into Baltimore Harbor, we were unaware of the fate of our sister schooners, but were thrilled to see the tall masts and yards of the big Swedish four-masted bark *Abraham Rydberg* at the end of the harbor. She had come in from South America. It was a sight to give a lift to the heart of a true sailor.

Once we were cleared by the port doctor, customs, and immigration, we had but one thought in mind: to telephone our loved ones and tell them we were alive and well. I told my mother I would soon be home and would discover what my role would be after I had seen her. To me, it seemed the beginning of another great adventure.

We put rat guards on our docklines to make it difficult for rats to leave the ship by that route, and then ran out the gangplank to make it easy for them to leave like gentlemen. As for our other creatures, I presume they were hoisted out with the cargo. I was not going to miss having to shake my bedclothes each time I got into my bunk, kick my shoes before putting them on, and be careful where I put my hands at all times. One morning a tarantula had stared at me from my wash basin. I wonder if he made his way ashore?

The shipping commissioner came aboard to pay us off, and the crew, bags already packed, left immediately. Bob and I had decided to spend one more night aboard and were walking up Pratt Street to do some shopping when suddenly a barroom door opened and old Martin stepped out.

"Hey Bob, hey Bowker, come in and have a drink. We all want to buy you a drink."

It had been our policy never to take a drink with the crew, and Bob and I started a polite refusal.

"I know you don't drink with the crew," said Martin, "but we are no longer a crew. We have been talking about you fellows and want to buy you one drink. We don't want you to stay. We don't want you to buy us a drink. We want to tell you that you are two damn good men and we'll ship with you any time, if we meet again."

We accepted that drink, as offered, and I will always feel it was one of the finest compliments that ever came my way. Those old hardbitten squareheads did not often hand out compliments to their officers, and it gave us a real lift.

The next day I shook hands with Captain Decker and said goodbye to Mrs. Decker with some regret. She and I had had many long conversations, and I got some insight into the lonely life of a shipmaster's wife. Even coastwise captains were often away for over a year between visits home, and their wives shouldered burdens not expected of the average housewife. This may have some bearing on the fact that many a shipmaster found his wife had steered his sons into other walks of life before he knew what was going on. I'm afraid many a captain was an unwelcome intruder on the domestic scene, upon the infrequent occasions of his visits home. The autocrat of the quarterdeck might rage around and give orders for a few weeks, but peace would settle upon the household once he departed.

As we left the *Herbert L. Rawding*, we all knew our lives would be vastly altered. Captain Decker commanded steamships throughout the war; Bob Robinson joined the navy and was lost before the year was out; Eddie Moran served in both the navy and merchant marine. For my own part, I shipped as seaman in a tanker during most of 1942, went to Officers' Training School, obtained my third mate's license, and served in this capacity aboard a troopship and an ammunition ship.

The War Years, 1942-1945 • 6

Shortly after we paid off from the *Rawding* on 25 March 1942, she was acquired by the Intercontinental Steamship Lines, Inc., of New York. Arthur W. Schoultz was president of this firm, which does not appear to have ever owned a steamship, but operated at least five schooners.

The *Rawding*'s subsequent career gives credence to rumors of profiteering heard about Intercontinental Steamship Lines, Inc. The captain and owner of a schooner sold to the company at an inflated price told me he took his money and, in spite of an offer by Captain Schoultz to "make me rich," returned to Nova Scotia in some fear for his life.[14]

On 14 April 1942 the *Herbert L. Rawding* was issued a warrant to carry general cargo from Baltimore to Barranquilla, Colombia. By 1 June Intercontinental Steamship Lines had applied to the War Shipping Administration for permission to carry cargo to South Africa for American African Overseas, Ltd. About the same time American African Overseas wrote to John W. Mann of the War Shipping Administration that they were about to purchase the *Herbert L. Rawding* from Emory Sexton of New York, "who are the authorized agents of the above named vessel," and stated that

the Intercontinental Steamship Lines, Inc., had no authority to apply for a warrant for the vessel.

Eventually Mr. Mann wrote to Intercontinental to find out who actually owned the *Herbert L. Rawding* and refused to take further action until that concern could prove intention to purchase the vessel from Herbert L. Rawding, Inc., or act as agent of that corporation. On 22 June Captain Schoultz wired Mr. Mann that he would libel the *Herbert L. Rawding* if she were sold to or through Emory Sexton, since he had been assured that the owners would sell her to Intercontinental Steamship and he had already contracted freights for the vessel. Captain Schoultz added on 29 June 1942, "We have had purchase agreement with owners since April and finally arranged details. No other direct purchasers except thru ship brokers without authority." It was 24 July before Captain Schoultz was able to produce an agreement of sale between the owners of the *Herbert L. Rawding* and Intercontinental Steamship Lines, Inc.

Intercontinental then requested warrants to load the *Herbert L. Rawding* for Capetown, South Africa. These warrants were issued 29 July 1942. About this time the Maritime Commission began to inquire about the freight rates Intercontinental was charging shippers and notified them that they should observe the rates established by the U.S.A./South Africa Conference. A representative of the East Asiatic Company had called to say the Caragol-Clarke Company, Inc., which had chartered the *Rawding* from Intercontinental Steamship Lines, was demanding ninety dollars per ton on 320,000 board feet of lumber. This was three times the approved rate.

After some correspondence, East Asiatic was informed that the maximum they could be charged was forty-five dollars per 1,000 board feet, plus a surcharge of 30 percent. Caragol-Clarke replied that they were not interested in doing business. Captain Schoultz was asked for an explanation and, when it was not immediately forthcoming, the War Shipping Administration threatened to revoke the warrants and invoke penalties.

Another complaint was filed by Inge & Company, a New York firm doing business for the East Asiatic Company. They had been quoted ninety dollars per ton on fifty tons of steel plate for South Africa. There was also a consignment of machinery. So pressed were the consignees for this material that they cabled consent to load at the ninety dollar rate. Inge & Company, however, made out affidavits which were forwarded to the War Shipping Administration.

For some reason, in mid-August 1942 the Isbrandtsen Steamship Company, Inc., was asked to report on the seaworthiness of the *Herbert L. Rawding*. They replied that the vessel was in good condition and should be loaded without delay. At this time the *Herbert L. Rawding* was lying in Baltimore while her fate was being decided among parties in Washington, New York, and South Africa. By 25 August Captain Schoultz, evidently frightened by the threat to tie up the *Rawding*, had

called Mr. Mann to deny any knowledge of the rates being charged by Caragol-Clarke, and warned that firm to conform to the rates in effect. As of this date, no cargo had actually been loaded aboard the *Herbert L. Rawding*. It seems that this furor alerted the Maritime Commission that an eye should be kept on small shipowners with an urge to profiteer on war conditions.

Intercontinental Steamship Lines, Inc., became an object of suspicion. They are said to have lost four out of five schooners they sent to sea during the war, and never delivered a cargo.

Any person serving in a merchant vessel in 1942 knew that a sailing vessel had little chance of making a voyage across the Atlantic. The German submarine fleet was everywhere, and steamships were sunk by the hundreds. What chance did a lone sailor have to wander across the sea? Some voyages were made, but a schooner was pathetically helpless. It is a strange phenomenon, but even Nazi submarine commanders showed a special humanity toward the crews of sailing vessels they were forced to sink. Perhaps because such craft were often encountered in lonely parts of the ocean and did not carry radio transmitters, a submarine would surface, give the crew a few minutes to get away in their boat, and destroy the schooner by shellfire or planted bombs. On occasion, a submarine commander would even provide a crew with some supplies as they set out on their ocean trek toward survival.

It may be that government employees were purposely putting roadblocks in the path of Intercontinental and other sailing vessel owners. If so, it was not entirely successful, for most of the sailing vessels that ventured upon wartime seas were lost. The four-master *Lillian E. Kerr* sailed into the middle of a convoy and was run down with the loss of all hands. The four-masters *Reine Marie Stewart*,

James E. Newsom, and *Albert F. Paul* were sunk by submarines, as was the steel three-master *Wawaloam*. There were others, and a number that foundered or ran aground.

Throughout September 1942 there were letters between the U.S. Maritime Commission and the U.S.A./South Africa Conference. It seems that Captain Schoultz had become elusive, and there were fears that he would load his vessels and slip out before legal steps could be taken to stop them. In mid-October, Mr. Hallett wrote to the Warrants Section of the War Shipping Administration and finished with the following words: "We believe that this carrier must be watched rather closely to see that he does not exceed the maximum rates authorized for this trade." Mr. Hallett was proven correct, as a letter from him to Intercontinental, dated 17 December 1942, attests: "Our records show that the *Herbert L. Rawding* sailed from Baltimore on October 20, 1942 for Capetown, South Africa with 1504 tons of commercial cargo, although we have not as yet received a filing of rates to cover this sailing. These rates should have been on file with this Division no later than November 20, 1942 pursuant to the rules and regulations . . . ."

Captain Schoultz had managed to slip the *Herbert L. Rawding* out to sea without complying with these directives, but she experienced trouble 400 miles out from New York and was brought in to a Carolina port. Then she was taken to Norfolk, Virginia, where her cargo was discharged. She had nine feet of water in her hold, and approximately 25 percent of her cargo had been damaged. A general average was declared, and after repairs she was expected to sail again for South Africa.

The warrants on both the *Constellation* and *Herbert L. Rawding* would expire on 28 July 1943, and a great push was made to get both vessels to sea by that date. On 30 July Captain Schoultz notified the Warrants Section, War Shipping Administration, that both vessels had sailed to destinations and requested new warrants. The *Constellation* was issued a new warrant for Aruba, but about 16 July sailed directly to Bermuda, where she was piled up on the reefs. The *Herbert L. Rawding* sailed for Capetown, South Africa, but she again experienced trouble and her master put in to Charleston, South Carolina, for repairs.

This was the end for Intercontinental Steamship Lines. Thirty-three shippers who had placed cargo aboard the *Rawding* removed their property and had it forwarded to South Africa by steamship. Captain Schoultz quietly closed down his office in New York and disappeared.

An article in the 22 October 1943 *New York Herald Tribune* was headlined, "Skipper of Sailing Fleet Accused of Taking $14,069 Insurance Fee." The Republic Chemical Corporation had put cargo valued at $36,500 aboard the *Rawding*. For this, aside from the freight money, they had paid Intercontinental Steamship Lines, Inc., $14,069.44 for insurance that was never paid to the insurance company. Upon his arrest, Captain Schoultz admitted appropriating the money and also that he had overcharged the company $2,000.

When it is considered that the thirty-three companies, including Vicks, Bristol-Myers, Miles Laboratory, and Colgate-Palmolive-Peet, had placed cargo valued at over $80,000 aboard the *Rawding*, Captain Schoultz must have collected a tidy fortune before his apprehension.

On 20 June 1944 the *New York Journal of Commerce* listed the *Rawding* for sale by the General Credit Corporation for $42,500, but there were no takers at that price, and the vessel lay in Charleston until 1945.

Captain Rodway Commands the *Herbert L. Rawding*, 1945-1947 • 7

The man who revived the *Herbert L. Rawding* after her ignominious wartime service was Captain Alex Rodway. Born in 1898 in the little village of Kingwell, on Long Island, Placentia Bay, Newfoundland, Captain Rodway was born to the sea. As soon as he was big enough, his father took him fishing, but Alec, as he is known, tired of that and could see little future in pulling codfish from the depths. He shipped in a schooner from Harbour Buffet, the main port on the island at that time, and began a career in vessels in the hard trade carrying salt cod to Spain and Portugal and returning with salt.

Winter and summer these schooners, mostly two- and three-masters, plied the North Atlantic. Fighting fog and snow, pack ice and gales, these small craft traversed some of the worst seas and weather one can imagine. A number of these vessels disappeared without a trace, and there were many tales of dramatic rescues. Captain Rodway survived fifty-two of these voyages. In 1921, at the age of twenty-one, he took charge of the schooner *Edith Pardy*, 84 tons register. In the schooner *Elizabeth Rodway* he made trips to Italy, and commanded another called *La Berge* in the coastwise trade.

In 1934 Captain Rodway went to Sweden and purchased a three-masted schooner called *Stina*, but after a few trips she foundered. Late in 1935 he went to New York, where he purchased the four-master *R.R. Govin* for Alberto Wareham, Ltd. He sailed this vessel to Labrador to load fish, but the owners felt she was too large for their business and sold her to Monroe Export, Ltd., of St. John's.

Still on the lookout for a large schooner, Captain Rodway got word that big schooners could be bought for a song at Boothbay Harbor, Maine. Away he went and purchased the *Mabel A. Frye*, a four-master of 1,151 gross tons. He sailed to Turks Island and brought a salt cargo to Sydney, Nova Scotia. The vessel had not been drydocked in years, but he thought he could earn enough in a few trips to put her in shape and replace the old sails. He loaded a cargo of coal for Harbour Grace, Newfoundland. In Captain Rodway's words: "We ran into one storm after another and got blown about 200 miles off the coast of Newfoundland. By now our ship was leaking and the pumps got choked up. We thought this was the end, but after a few days adrift, the steamer *American Merchant* came by, picked us up and took us to New York. We saw the *Frye* go down."

Captain Alex Rodway (second from left) poses with the crew of the schooner MABEL A. FRYE, 1936. The others are, left to right, John Rodway, Thomas Burton, Fred Wareham, George Slade, and Cleverly Ingraham.
(Courtesy Captain R.A. Rodway)

After the loss of the *Mabel A. Frye*, Captain Rodway spent a few years trading locally around Newfoundland, Labrador, and the Canadian coasts. The war was drawing to a close when, late in 1944, his brother Charles, who was superintendent of the Seaman's Institute in Portland, Maine, told him that the *Herbert L. Rawding* was for sale and sent along an advertisement from a nautical paper. Captain Alec discussed the matter with Freeman Wareham, who sent him to Charleston, South Carolina. Here he found the vessel to be in good condition and, after a bit of hard bargaining, purchased her in January 1945 for $18,000.[15]

Immediately a crew was shipped down from Newfoundland, sail was bent, a bit of line may have been rove off, and the *Rawding* set off to load salt at Turks Island for Harbour Buffet. When Captain Rodway sailed his big schooner right into Harbour Buffet, she was the largest sailing vessel ever seen by many of the inhabitants. She lay at anchor and discharged much of the cargo directly into trading vessels that would deliver it to small outports for curing fish. Considering that freight rates were about $18 per ton on her roughly 1,900 tons of salt, and that Mr. Wareham owned both ship and cargo, the $34,000 freight paid for the

**Mr. Freeman Wareham, last owner of the
HERBERT L. RAWDING.**
(Photo by author)

ship, with a tidy profit to boot. It seems likely that most of the provisions for the African voyage were still aboard, for there had been only a shipkeeper aboard for several months. Mr. Wareham had made a good bargain.

After the salt was discharged, the *Rawding* made three trips from North Sydney, Nova Scotia, to Port aux Basques, Newfoundland. With a bit of attention to weather, and a good, fair wind, this was only an eighteen to twenty-four-hour run. While the freight rate was only $4 a ton, it amounted to an $8,000 freight. With 1,900 tons below, Captain Rodway would take a chance on a few hundred tons on deck; the Plimsoll mark must have been under water.

About this time it was decided to put engines in the ship. The *Rawding* took one last load of coal down to St. John's. Mr. Wareham purchased two huge, war-surplus Clark diesel engines of 350 horsepower, weighing twenty-one tons each. While negotiations were under way for the installation, Captain Rodway sent down the topmasts and unshipped the jibboom, as he planned to use the engines for the main propulsion. While Mr. Wareham was still seeking a contract to install the engines at a reasonable rate, he sent the vessel to Turks Island for one more cargo of salt and, when that was discharged, she proceeded to Pictou, Nova Scotia, where a good deal for the engine installation was arranged with the Ferguson Industries yard. The engines were shipped there and, as soon as the vessel arrived, preparations commenced for their installation.

Captain Victor Butler, who was also born on Long Island, Newfoundland was sent to Pictou along with Freeman Wareham's eleven-year-old son Eric. Captain Butler was a versatile man who had turned his hand to many trades: hunting and fishing, a spell as a street car operator, trading in small schooners around the coast, carpentry, and mechanics. He had installed and repaired engines aboard vessels owned and operated by Alberto Wareham, Ltd., so Mr. Wareham wanted him to supervise the installation aboard the *Rawding*.

The shipyard did not have a crane that could hoist such large engines aboard, so they had to be disassembled and the pieces reassembled in the hold of the ship. In a letter to me, Captain Butler discussed the job.

> We then docked the ship to have her bottom painted and caulked and shaft logs, shafts, struts and all underwater fittings installed. It was a complicated job as both tail shafts were thirty nine feet long and had to be properly aligned with the engines.

We also installed a diesel lighting plant and batteries, also fuel tanks to contain three thousand gallons and all necessary equipment for a twin engine installation, while taking care of all the regulations required by the Steam Ship Inspector and [insurance] investigator, who was continually examining every part of the vessel for seaworthiness. The anchor chains were hauled out on the deck and X-rays were taken to determine if they were trustworthy.

In order to make space, the spanker mast had been removed and Captain Rodway had the fore, main, and mizzen shortened by twelve feet. This, of course, meant that the sails also had to be recut and all rigging shortened. By the time all this was accomplished, the poor old schooner looked more like a barge than a sailing vessel. Near where the spanker had risen, two stubby exhaust stacks stuck up in the air, just forward of the cabin.

It was well along in December before all was ready and they made a trial run. Captain Butler reported she logged 10.4 nautical miles per hour. There was already ice forming in Pictou Harbor, and it was time to move along.

Captain Rodway had hoped to get a cargo of potatoes from Prince Edward Island to Cuba. From

The HERBERT L. RAWDING lies at St. John's, Newfoundland, early in 1946. The snow-covered hills and ice-filled harbor must have made a trip to Turks Island, Bahamas, for salt sound attractive to Captain Rodway and his crew.
(Courtesy Captain Adrian K. Lane)

The **HERBERT L. RAWDING** making sail after being towed out from
St. John's, Newfoundland, by **H.M.C.S. RIVERTON, 12 March 1946.**
The jet of steam attests to the efforts of the donkey engine in the cold
air as she gets under way for Turks Island.
(Courtesy Captain Adrian K. Lane)

there he would have run over to Turks Island to take a salt cargo home, but the deal fell through. Instead, the vessel was chartered to carry lumber to Alexandria, Egypt, and Cyprus.

The captain told me he carried slightly over a million board feet at a prepaid freight of $35 per thousand, or some $35,000. Remembering the *Rawding*'s crankiness, I asked how much of a deckload she carried.

"Oh, about seven feet," the captain replied.

"Didn't it make her a bit cranky?"

"Yes. But I think when she rolled down far enough the deckload used to float her back. You know, she was loaded up in kind of a funny way. Most of the lumber came down from up north by train, and it was covered with snow. But when we arrived there [Halifax], there was about four carloads of nice dry lumber on the dock. That went right in the bottom and all that heavy lumber that came from up north and was covered with ice and snow went right on the top, so she wasn't very well balanced.

"Anyhow, I left Halifax and the wind was from the west and blowin' quite hard. We runned her off. We had the mains'l and the fore on her, that night. Blowin' quite hard. Had the power goin'. We were off to the southard of Sable Island.

"Next day we were battin' along quite good but then the wind come around to the nor'west. Oh, there come a real gale of it and we were runnin' off before it. I had a fellow, Tommy Ashbourne. He was only a young fellow, was mate with me. He'd just got his ticket in Halifax and he wanted a job. So I wanted a mate and he come down, and I said 'Yes, alright.' So Tommy come. We were running her this night and she'd swing, and she was goin' down and I thought to myself 'I wonder . . . I don't suppose she can trip because the lumber'l float her back again if she goes far enough,

The RAWDING departs St. John's for Turks Island, Bahamas, on her last voyage without engines, 12 March 1946. She is what was called a "bald-headed schooner," an apt term for a schooner without topmasts.
(Courtesy Captain Adrian K. Lane)

and I was wonderin', if she goes far enough would she still keep on, but she did, an' I kept her before it. We made a good trip. She was nine days from Halifax to Gibraltar, but there was one night we laid to when it blowed hard from the nor'eastard.''

The *Rawding* arrived at Alexandria with her cargo intact and proceeded to Cyprus to discharge the balance. While at Cyprus, Captain Rodway looked around for a return cargo. One offer was a load of bauxite, but the insurance company refused to let him load that on the grounds that material it contains is injurious to wooden ships. The British Government wanted him to carry a hundred people to Madagascar, but there were no facilities aboard for handling passengers. Captain Rodway cabled back, ''I ABSOLUTELY REFUSE!''

Laden with salt from Turks Island, the HERBERT L. RAWDING returns to Harbour Buffet on her last voyage under sail alone, the last of her kind. Though shorn of her topmasts and long jibboom, she retains the dignified appearance common to ships of sail. (Courtesy Captain W.J.L. Parker)

The HERBERT L. RAWDING sits on the railway at Ferguson Industries, Pictou, Nova Scotia, in the fall of 1946. The spanker mast has been removed to accommodate the engines, the three remaining masts have been shortened, and the jibboom has been removed. She is now more of a motor-sailer than a schooner, but the aging wooden hull can not long endure the vibration of the huge engines and the long shafts running through struts attached to the planking and frames.
(Courtesy Freeman Wareham)

At last a charter was fixed to go to Cadiz, Spain, and take salt to Newfoundland. The old schooner started chugging her way toward Cadiz, but ran into a violent westerly gale off Malta. Being light, the vessel made little headway. As the seas grew to mountainous height, she would thrust her bows at the sky and then pitch toward the bottom, throwing her stern in the air and exposing her propellers, which would shake the entire ship. She did not seem to make any appreciable water, but it was decided to turn around and run before the gale under bare poles.

Eventually the wind moderated and the seas went down. Resuming her course, the *Rawding* made her way to Cadiz, apparently little worse for her experience. But damage had been done.

Loading a full cargo of salt, the vessel stopped at Gibraltar for bunker oil and headed for the open sea in June 1947. Three days out of Gibraltar she was overtaken by a heavy nor'easter and began to leak badly. She was logy and yawed. An attempt to heave to failed, so she was run off before it, and the water in the hold continually gained on the pumps. Eventually, dissolving salt clogged the pumps. Things were looking pretty grim when the American liberty ship *Robert W. Hart* arrived on the scene. The *Rawding*'s crew put over her boat and made it safely to the steamship, where Captain Quigley and his crew made the distressed mariners comfortable.[16]

The *Hart* stayed in the vicinity for about an hour and a half as the *Rawding* settled. Finally the schooner's stern went under, her bows rose in the air, and the last four-masted schooner to carry a cargo on the Atlantic went to the bottom about 500 miles off Cape St. Vincent.

Colby Eyre, John Lance, second engineer Freeman Gilbert, donkeyman
Calvin Gilbert, and Arthur Way pose on the RAWDING's after cabin
while she is hauled out at Pictou, Nova Scotia. Partially obscured by
the men is the exhaust stack for the port engine; the starbord engine
exhaust is at right. Note the engine room ventilator at left.

(Courtesy Freeman Wareham)

BUREAU VERITAS

District Bath, Me.

Surveyor's N°

CLASSIFICATION REPORT

SECTION N°

Account for 4th Quarter 19 19

WOODEN VESSEL built under (1) Ordinary Survey.

Name of Vessel Herbert L. Rawding — Flag American

Description (2) — Method of propulsion / Number of screws — Number of masts, and rig Sch. 4 Mast

Builder Stockton Yard Inc.

Place of construction Stockton Springs, Maine

Keel laid Dec. 19 18, Launched Sept. 25 19 19, Completed Sept. 19 19

Owners Atlantic Coast Co., L. K. Thurlow, Manager — Port of registry Boston, Mass

Captain John V. McKown — Date of captain's certificate — Signal letters LSFD

Description of timber Hardwood bottom, Spruce top — Bolting Black Iron, Galv. No. 21885

Class and term 3/3 A 15 yrs. from Oct. 1, 1919 — Computation of term in years — Wood Special survey / Bolting / Salting

PRINCIPAL DIMENSIONS

	BY RULES	REGISTERED (Customs)
Length between perpendiculars	201 7/10	
Breadth moulded	38-5	
Depth: top of keel top/upper deck beams at side	21-9	
of hold (from top of floors to top of deck beams at centre)	0	
Tonnage: gross		1219
net		1109
under upper deck		

Summer freeboard (centre of disc) by British/French rules

Measured from the upper edge of the deck line at __ (3) deck.

(4) Statutory deck line __ above the level of __ (3) deck.

Depth of keel __ maximum load draft (5)

Approximate deadweight on summer freeboard (centre of disc)

Maximum Number of cabin passengers or 'tween-deck passengers

Length of principal superstructures (between perpendiculars) Poop __ Bridge __ Forecastle __ (or raised deck)

Number of decks — Two

Number of tiers of hold beams — 50

Sheathing

When put on

When bottom last caulked Sept. 1919

Number of hatchways on upper deck three

Dimensions of hatches 11-14 Upper / 11-17 Lower

Electric lightning? Yes — Wireless?

Night signalling

Special fire extinguishing apparatus

Diameter of chain cable 1 ¾ inches

Sketch showing internal subdivision, length and profile of superstructures and raised decks

Sketch showing superstructures and cargo hatches, and their dimensions.

(1) Special or ordinary. — (2) Cargo or fishing vessel, trawler, tug, etc. — (3) Upper, or second deck. — (4) If the freeboard is calculated by British rules. — (5) Maximum draft from bottom of keel to centre of disc.

SCANTLINGS OF HULL

Longitudinal Numeral L × B × D

Transverse Numeral B + D

Proportion L/B __ L/D

ITEM	NUMBER OF PIECES	SCANTLINGS MOULDING | SIDING	DESCRIPTION OF TIMBER and YEARS ASSIGNED	FASTENINGS METAL	DIAMETER	TYPE	TREENAILS
Keel	10	12x14	White Oak	Iron	1 1/8	1½ 4" shoe	Locust
Stem		14x20	" "				
Sternpost		16x20	" "				
Floors		12x14	Hard wood				
Timbers at light water line		11x12x13					
Timbers at covering board		8x11	Spruce top				
Centre keelson		7x14 10 pcs.	Fir Fastened with 1½ iron				
Bilge keelson		7x14 5	" " "	1½	1 1/8 iron		
Deadwood		14x16	Oak				
Main transom	3	12x14	Fir				
Deck clamps		10x14	"				
Thick-strakes		10x12 10x13	10x14				
Deck beams	50	10x14	Upper Deck				
Knees horizontal	82	Hanging Knees from 8" to 10" thick					
Knees vertical		square fastened part from the outside					
Hold beams	50	12x12 12x14					
Pillars		Stringers under beams 9x12					
Covering boards		6x16 or rail					
Lockstrakes		12x12 10x12					
Waterways		12x13					
Ceiling		10x14 10x13 10x12	Fir fastened with 1½ 1 1/8 iron				
Spirketting		Chock 9x10 on rail					
Garboard		8x14 7x13 6x13	Edge bolted to keel 1" iron				
Bilges		4½x14 4½x13 4½x12					
Wales		4½x7 4½x8 4½x9					
Outside planking		Fir 4½ thick					
Deck planking		4x4 Pine, Upper 4x6 Lower, Fir					

Timber and spacing __ 30"

Number of pieces in midship timber __ 14 pcs.

Deck beams and spacing __ 3ft. 9" on center

Number and position of pillars

Metal of sheathing (and weight) __ "A" __ Height to which it extends

EQUIPMENT   3

Longitudinal numeral . . . .
Half capacity of principal superstructures (forecastle, raised deck, poop) . . . .
Quarter capacity of other superstructures (deck houses) . . . .
Numeral for hawsers and warps . . . . .
Numeral for anchors and chains (steamers) . . . .

			weight(t) — including stock	Chain cables (studded)	Diameter. 1⅛ " Total length 180 fathom Nº of lengths. .
Anchors	Bower {	1ˢᵗ (pattern) 4000 2ⁿᵈ 4000 3ʳᵈ			
	Stream anchor (pattern) Kedge 760		Hawsers and Towline	5½ 110 fathom 5 200 " 5 150 " 4½ 200 "

		LENGTH	HEAD	DIAMETER		LENGTH	ARM	DIAMETER
	Fore mast	98	10½	27	Fore yard			
	Main mast	"		26	Main yard			
	Mizen mast. . . .	"		"	Crossjuck			
	Bowsprit	46		26	Fore topsail yard . .			
Masts and Rigging	Jibboom	57		1717	Main topsail yard . .			
	Fore topmast . . .	50		15	Mizen topsail yard .			
	Main topmast . . .	"		14	Topgallant yards . .			
	Mizen topmast . .	"		"	Mizen topgallant yard .			
	Fore topgallant mast .				Fore and main gaffs.	39-8		
	Main topgallant mast				Mizen gaff . . . . Spanker boom	64		17

	FOREMAST	MAINMAST	MIZENMAST
Shrouds and stays, Diam.	4"	4"	4"
Topmast stays, circumference	2½"		
Backstays and topgallant stays, circumference.	3"	3"	3"

Rudder	Rudderstock of **White Oak**		diameter 18"
	Pintles, of _____ number _____ 3		diameter 3½
	Thickness of back pieces _____ steering leads of		diameter
	Type of steering gear _____ **Robinson**		
	Auxiliary gear		

Windlass. { Diameter of windlass (exclusive of lining) . . . . . . wood
Diameter of spindle . . . . . . 5½ wood

Number of boats, material, type, number of davits **22 ft. Power   One dory 14 ft.**

Ventilators. { Number of ventilators. — Diameters. — Height of coaming and cowl. — Goose-neck and mushroom ventilators

Hand pumps. { Number and type of pumps (delivery a box per bore) **One steam wrecking 6"   4" pipe**
Position **Forward**
Pump wells

OUTFIT AND SPARE GEAR FOR HULL

Carpenter's tools **1 set**
Caulking tools **1 "**
Relieving tackle for rudder **One**
Rearing chain shackles **Yes**
Shackles for chain cables
Fire buckets and hatches **fitted with**
Stretching screws

Spare sails for square rigged vessels	Fore topmast staysail. Jib. Mainsail. Foresail. Topsail complete. Topgallantsail complete. Fore topmast staysail.	**One jib** **Fore sail topsail**
Spare sails for fore-and-aft rigged vessels	Trysail. Jib. Fore and main staysail.	

For sailing vessels only.

Spare spars for vessels with fidded masts. { (a) Spare suitable for topmast, or topsail yard and topgallant mast. (b) Spare suitable for topgallant yard.

Spare spars for vessels with pole masts. { (a) Spare suitable for topgallant mast and lower topsail yard. (b) Spare suitable for topgallant yard.

Remarks on workmanship &c :
Material, workmanship and fastening good

2 sets of pointers aft, 12x14 3 breasthooks
3 sets "   "   forward "   "
                                 fastened with 1 1/8 1½ iron

Outside planking: First garboard edge bolted to keel; all treenails used outside in planking, locust in bilge and topsides, half go through. All butts bolted and wood ends, yellow metal spikes and butt bolts used to light water line.
Well caulked Salting full

Number of visits. **5**

At **Stockton Springs** the **Nov. 14th, 1919**

Certificate.	115.00	115.00
Fees	343.80	343.80
Days of absence	5 days	30
Travelling expenses, etc . .	30.00	488.80
Total. .	$488.80	

SURVEYOR,
James H. Cameron
Salter Img
asst. Chester & Pasca
Rockport

The following list has been compiled from the *Rawding*'s Registers and Enrollments on file at the National Archives in Washington, D.C.

1919
25 September—Captain John V. McKown took the vessel from Stockton Springs, Maine, to Newport News, Virginia. The Atlantic Coast Company, a subsidiary of Crowell & Thurlow of Boston, was her owner. *8 October*—Captain Charles Glaesel took command.
1920
3 May—Captain M.D. Saunders took command.
1921
26 January—Captain John J. Irons listed as master.
18 July—Captain George W. Higbee listed as master.
8 November—Captain J.F. Skolfield became master until 1925.
1925
1 April—New England Maritime Company of Boston now listed as owner; Captain Jose P. DaCosta master.
1 December—Captain M.C. Decker listed as master.
1926
26 February—E.G. Joslin listed as master, but in other documents listed as secretary. Perhaps Captain Decker was not present and Joslin filled out the papers.
12 October—Captain E.G. Barlow listed as master.
1927
4 May—Captain W.E. Rutledge listed as master.
1929
28 May—Captain M.C. Decker again became master.

Ownership of the vessel changed: Lewis K. Thurlow owned 2/64, Ella P. Thurlow owned 62/64; management remained with Crowell & Thurlow.
1931
17 February—Captain Decker brought the vessel to Boothbay Harbor, Maine, to be laid up with others of the Crowell & Thurlow fleet. Her document, dated 17 February 1931, was surrendered at New York on 19 April 1937 with a note stating "papers deposited Oct. 1931."
1936
14 December—"License renewed for one year." Captain Robert W. Rickson took oath as master.
1937
19 April—Kiraco Transportation Corp., New York, now owner; Kiraco Transportation Corp. mortgager, Herman B. Baruch mortgagee for $15,000. Captain R.W. Rickson master. *3 June*—Captain R.W. Rickson master, and president of Kiraco Transportation Corp.
1939
25 January—Captain R.W. Rickson, New York, owner and master. *29 November*—Captain Harold G. Foss, Boston, owner and master. *16 December*—Captain George W. Hopkins listed as master.
1940
1 January—Captain H.G. Foss mortgager, Joseph E. O'Connell and William L. Thompson mortgagees for $60,000. *4 November*—The Herbert L. Rawding, Inc., Boston, owner, with Andrew B. Sides president. Captain Winsor W. Torrey master. *5 December*—Captain M.C. Decker listed as master.

1942
8 April—Andrew B. Sides managing owner with 2/15;
together with Joseph E. O'Connell of Newton,
Massachusetts, 6/15; William L. Thompson of Winchester,
Massachusetts, 6/15; and Joseph W. Woods of Ipswich,
Massachusetts, 1/15. Captain M.C. Decker listed as
master. *15 August*—Intercontinental Steamship Lines, Inc.,
owner, Arthur W. Schoultz, Brooklyn, New York,
president. *27 October*—Captain N.G. Ibsen listed as master.
1943
24 June—Intercontinental Steamship Lines, Inc., mortgager,
Bankers Commercial Corp. mortgagee for $85,000. Captain
Charles A.K. Bertun master.
1944
6 March—General Credit Corp., New York, owner, W.
Trebling secretary. *26 March*—U.S. Marshall Bill of Sale
recorded with note, ''see other mortgage, $50,600, endorsed
Dec. 9, 1942.''
1945
27 March—Document surrendered by Robert Jacob, Inc.,
owner, Kalman Greenberg secretary. *27 March*—
Alberto Wareham, Ltd., Arnold's Cove, Newfoundland,
purchased vessel for $18,000. Captain R. Alex Rodway
became master.
1947
10 June—Vessel foundered while owned by Alberto
Wareham, Ltd., and commanded by Captain R.A. Rodway.

Compiled from listings in the *New York Maritime Register*.
Errors and unreported passages may exist. Entrance and
clearance dates were not always reported in the register.

1919
Stockton, Maine, to Norfolk, Virginia—*27 Sept-Oct.*
Norfolk to Canary Islands—*Oct.-25 Nov.*
1920
Canary Islands to Buenos Aires, Argentina—*?-22 Jan.*
Buenos Aires to New York—*3 Feb.-22 Apr.*
Perth Amboy to Norfolk—
Norfolk to Lisbon, Portugal—*28 May-27 June*
Lisbon to Boston—*21 Aug.-3 Oct.*
Boston to Norfolk—*6 Nov.-*
1921
Hampton Roads to Portland—*?-14 Mar.*
Portland to Hampton Roads via New York—*18 Mar.-4 Apr.*
Norfolk to Providence—*15 Apr.-22 Apr.*
Providence to Hampton Roads—
Hampton Roads to Providence—*5 May-12 May*
Providence to Newport News—*May-22 May*
Newport News to Boston—*27 May-3 June*
Boston to Wilmington, North Carolina—*20 July-16 Aug.*
Wilmington To Jacksonville, Florida—
Jacksonville to Boston—*4 Oct.-15 Oct.*
Boston to Tampa, Florida—*11 Nov.-*
1922
Tampa to Baltimore—*24 Dec.-16 Jan.*
Norfolk to Boston—*?-8 Mar.*
Boston to Norfolk—*15 Mar.-11 Apr.*

Norfolk to Calais, Maine—*20 Apr.-*
Calais to Walton, Nova Scotia—
Walton to Norfolk—*26 May-11 June*
Norfolk to New London—*1 July-9 Aug.*
? to Baltimore—*?-15 Sept.*
Baltimore to Norfolk—*18 Sept.-25 Sept.*
Norfolk to Calais, Maine—
Calais to Walton—
Walton to Norfolk—*?-13 Dec.*
1923
Norfolk to Maine—*29 Dec.-Jan.*
Providence to Norfolk via New York—*?-31 Jan.*
Norfolk to New Haven—*2 Mar.-13 Apr.*
New Haven to Hampton Roads—
Newport News to Jacksonville—*19 Apr.-4 June*
Jacksonville to Boston—*30 June-19 July*
Boston to Port St. Joe, Florida—*?-16 Sept.*
Port St. Joe to Fall River—*10 Oct.-11 Nov.*
Fall River to Norfolk—*?-28 Dec.*
1924
Norfolk to Portland—*1 Jan.-20 Jan.*
Portland to Norfolk—*7 Feb.-14 Feb.*
Norfolk to Calais—*15 Mar.-*
Calais to Hillsboro, New Brunswick—*?-24 May*
Hillsboro to Norfolk—*?-14 June*
Norfolk to Tampa—*28 June-4 Aug.*
Tampa to Wilmington, North Carolina—*8 Aug.-27 Aug.*
Wilmington to Charleston—*19 Sept.-*
Charleston to San Juan—*12 Oct.-7 Nov.*
San Juan to Turks Island—*29 Nov.-4 Dec.*

1925
Turks Island to Boston via Norfolk in distress—*?-22 Feb.*
Boston to Baltimore—*5 Apr.-14 Apr.*
Baltimore to Tampa—
Tampa to Baltimore—*15 June-29 June*
Baltimore to Steuben, Maine—*27 Aug.-*
Steuben to Baltimore—*23 Sept.-*
Norfolk to Bangor—*1 Oct.-*
Portland to New York—*9 Nov.-*
New York (?) to Savannah—*?-25 Nov.*
Savannah to Miami—*16 Dec.-31 Dec.*
1926
Miami to Key West—*19 Feb.-?*
Key West to Miami—*?-28 Mar.*
Miami to New Bedford—*?-27 Apr.*
New Brunswick to Norfolk—*21 July-29 July*
Norfolk to Calais—*8 Aug.-9 Oct.*
Eastport to Parrsboro, Nova Scotia—*20 Oct.-*
Nova Scotia to Norfolk via Portland—*?-3 Dec.*
1927
Norfolk to Baltimore—*?-31 Jan.*
Baltimore to Searsport, Maine—*6 Feb.-*
Searsport to Hampton Roads—*?-4 Apr.*
Hampton Roads to Calais (?)—*6 Apr.-*
Calais to Hampton Roads—*?-14 June.*
Newport News to Calais—*23 July-27 Aug.*
Eastport to Miramichi, New Brunswick—*12 Sept.-23 Sept.*
Miramichi to Portland—*?-16 Oct.*
Portland to Puerto Rico—*6 Nov.-*
1928
Cabo Rojo, Puerto Rico, to Portland—*21 Dec.-14 Jan.*
Portland to Norfolk, stopped at Boston—*17 Feb.-29 Feb.*
Laid up at Boston—*Mar. 1928-May 1929*
1929
Boston to Charleston—*2 June-*
Charleston to Brunswick, Georgia—*28 June-1 July*
Brunswick to New York—*9 July-25 July*
New York to Hampton Roads(?)—*5 Aug.-*
Norfolk to Calais—*?-3 Sept.*
Eastport to Norfolk—*26 Sept.-5 Oct.*
Newport News to Turks Island—*26 Oct.-4 Nov.*
Turks Island to Boston—*?-21 Dec.*
1930
Boston to Mayaguez, Puerto Rico—*6 Apr.-21 Apr.*
Mayaguez to Boston—*17 May-June*

Boston to New York—*?-19 June*
New York to Boston—*27 June-*
Boston to Jacksonville—
Jacksonville to Portland—*1 Aug.-18 Aug.*
Portland to Newport News—*18 Oct.-*
Newport News to Guadeloupe—
1931
Pointe-a-Pitre, Guadeloupe, to Wilmington, North Carolina
   —*Jan.-16 Feb.*
Wilmington to New York—*3 Mar.-10 Mar.*
New York to Norfolk—*11 Apr.-*
Norfolk to New England—
New England to Norfolk—*?-25 May*
Norfolk to New England—*25 July-*
1932-1936
Laid up at Boothbay Harbor, Maine, until *Dec. 1936*
1937
Boothbay Harbor to Portland—*Dec.-2 Jan.*
Portland to Newcastle, New Brunswick—*9 June-*
Newcastle to New York—*10 July-22 Aug.*
New York to Portsmouth, New Hampshire—*14 Nov.-*
Portsmouth to Miami—*27 Nov.-16 Dec.*
Miami to Mobile—*?-30 Dec.*
1938
Mobile to Santiago, Cuba—*21 Jan.-7 Mar.*
Santiago to Jacksonville—
Jacksonville to San Juan—*11 May-26 May*
San Juan to Savannah—*17 June-27 June*
Savannah to Jacksonville—*2 Nov.-6 Nov.*
1939
Jacksonville to Norfolk—*1 Apr.-16 Apr.*
Newport News to Bermuda—*31 May-9 June*
Bermuda to Haiti—*20 June-8 July*
Haiti to Baltimore—*?-7 Aug.*
Baltimore to Norfolk—*4 Dec.-*
1940
Norfolk to Fort-de-France, Martinique—*25 Dec.-17 Jan.*
Fort-de-France to Turks Island—*?-20 Feb.*
Turks Island to Norfolk—*26 Feb.-8 Mar.*
Norfolk to Fort-de-France—*15 June-*
Fort-de-France to Aruba—
Aruba to Baltimore—*?-24 Oct.*
Baltimore to Norfolk—*15 Nov.-.*
Hampton Roads to Point-a-Pitre, Guadeloupe—
   13 Dec.-1 Jan.

1941
Point-a-Pitre to Las Piedras, Venezuela—
Las Piedras to Boston—*21 Feb.-22 Mar.*
Boston to Norfolk—*12 Apr.-21 Apr.*
Norfolk to Galion Bay, Martinique—*2 May-*
Galion Bay to Turks Island—
Turks Island to Yarmouth, Nova Scotia—*?-24 July*
Yarmouth to Sheet Harbor, Nova Scotia—
Sheet Harbor to New York—*28 Aug.-18 Sept.*
New York to Newport News—*7 Nov.-14 Nov.*
Hampton Roads to Fort-de-France, Martinique—
    24 Nov.-26 Dec.
1942
Fort-de-France to Cap-Haitien, Haiti—*17 Jan.-25 Jan.*
Cap-Haitien to Baltimore—*15 Mar.-23 Mar.*
Baltimore to Capetown, taken to Norfolk in distress—
    20 Oct.-
1943-1944
Norfolk to Capetown, taken to Charleston in distress—*July-*
Laid up at Charleston, *July 1943-Jan. 1945*
1945
Charleston to Turks Island—*Jan. 1945-*
Turks Island to Harbour Buffet, Newfoundland—
Harbour Buffet to North Sydney, Nova Scotia—
North Sydney to Port aux Basques, Newfoundland—
Port aux Basques to North Sydney—
North Sydney to Port aux Basques—
Port aux Basques to North Sydney—
North Sydney to Port aux Basques—
Port aux Basques to North Sydney—
North Sydney to St. John's—
1946
St. John's to Turks Island—
Turks Island to St. John's—
St. John's to Pictou, Nova Scotia—
Pictou to Halifax—
1947
Halifax to Alexandria, Egypt—
Alexandra to Cyprus—
Cyprus to Cadiz—
Cadiz to Newfoundland via Gibraltar, sank 500 miles off
    Cape St. Vincent, Spain—*?-10 June*

Modeling the *Herbert L. Rawding* at Mystic Seaport Museum

In 1979 Mystic Seaport Museum decided to add a model of one of the big four-masted schooners to the collections. Although a good set of plans for the *Helen Barnet Gring* was available, I suggested that the *Herbert L. Rawding* would make a fine candidate. She was a slightly different model and, to my eye, a better looking vessel. Among the most compelling reasons for choosing this vessel was the fact that, over the years, I had collected a fine set of photographs of and about the *Rawding*, some of the best of which were taken by Garrett I. Johnson, a New Jersey photographer who had planned to build a model himself.

Some years ago, I was given access to the quarters of the Gordon & Hutchins sail loft, on Commercial Wharf, Boston, which had been vacated when Mr. George Gordon died. The place had been somewhat vandalized, but I found a few old sail plans scattered around. One of these was an original Crowell & Thurlow sail plan for the *Herbert L. Rawding*.

Mrs. George H. Hopkins of Stockton Springs, Maine, made available the half model, supposedly used for the *Alcaeus Hooper*, the slightly larger sister of the *Rawding*. We felt that the *Rawding*'s model would have been nearly identical, so lines were taken from the *Hooper* model, by Maynard Bray, and adapted for the work in hand.

William S. Quincy, Mystic Seaport Museum model maker, drew up the plans to a scale of 3/16-inch to the foot. Over two hundred photogrpahs were available, taken from almost every angle, and Bill was able to scale off dimensions for detail drawings.

It seems that no matter how many photographs are taken about a ship, there is always some detail a model maker needs that hasn't been covered. A case in point was the steam capstan on the forecastle head. A number of our photos showed the area but, in all of them, the capstan was missing. Bill refused to add one until I proved it was there. Frantic letters went out to everyone we could think of who might have snapped a photo of our vessel. It was the ever reliable Charles S. Morgan who came up with what was needed.

We believe the following plans are as accurate as any plans for a four-masted schooner can be. Model makers wishing to purchase full-sized plans drawn to 3/16-inch scale should contact the Curatorial Office, Mystic Seaport Museum, Box 6000, Mystic, CT 06355-0990.

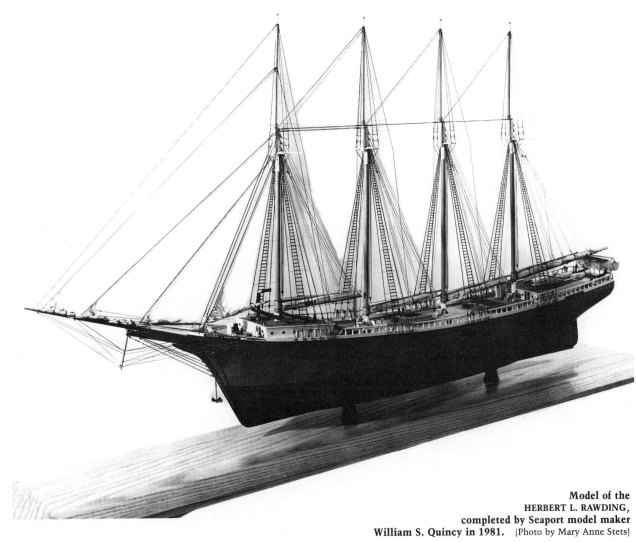

**Model of the
HERBERT L. RAWDING,
completed by Seaport model maker
William S. Quincy in 1981.** (Photo by Mary Anne Stets)

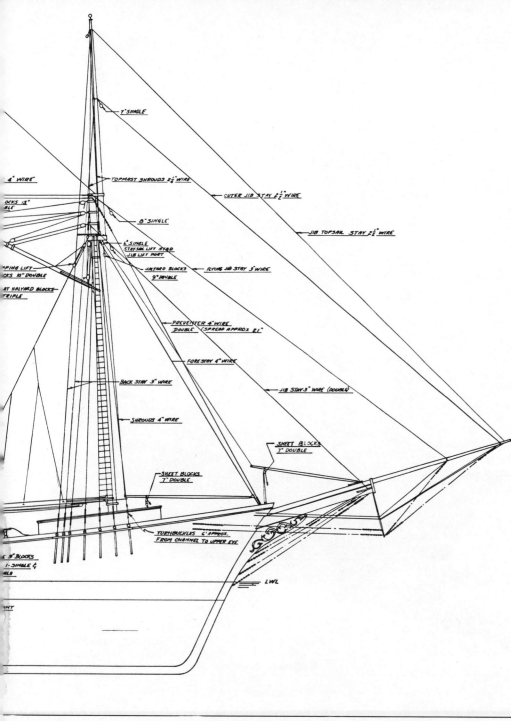

7" SINGLE

4" WIRE

TOPMAST SHROUDS 2½" WIRE

OUTER JIB STAY 2½" WIRE

OCKS 13"
LE

8" SINGLE

JIB TOPSAIL STAY 2½" WIRE

6" SINGLE
STAYSAIL LIFT ST'B'D
JIB LIFT PORT

PING LIFT
CKS 10" DOUBLE

HALYARD BLOCKS
9" DOUBLE

FLYING JIB STAY 3" WIRE

T HALYARD BLOCKS
TRIPLE

PREVENTER 4" WIRE
DOUBLE (SPREAD APPROX 21")

FORESTAY 4" WIRE

BACK STAY 3" WIRE

JIB STAY 3" WIRE (DOUBLE)

SHROUDS 4" WIRE

SHEET BLOCKS
7" DOUBLE

SHEET BLOCKS
7" DOUBLE

TURNBUCKLES 6" APPROX.
FROM CHANNEL TO UPPER EYE

LWL

9" BLOCKS
-SINGLE &
LE

NT

MYSTIC SEAPORT
MYSTIC   CONNECTICUT

SCHOONER
HERBERT L. RAWDING

DRAWN BY W S QUINCY   1980 - 81

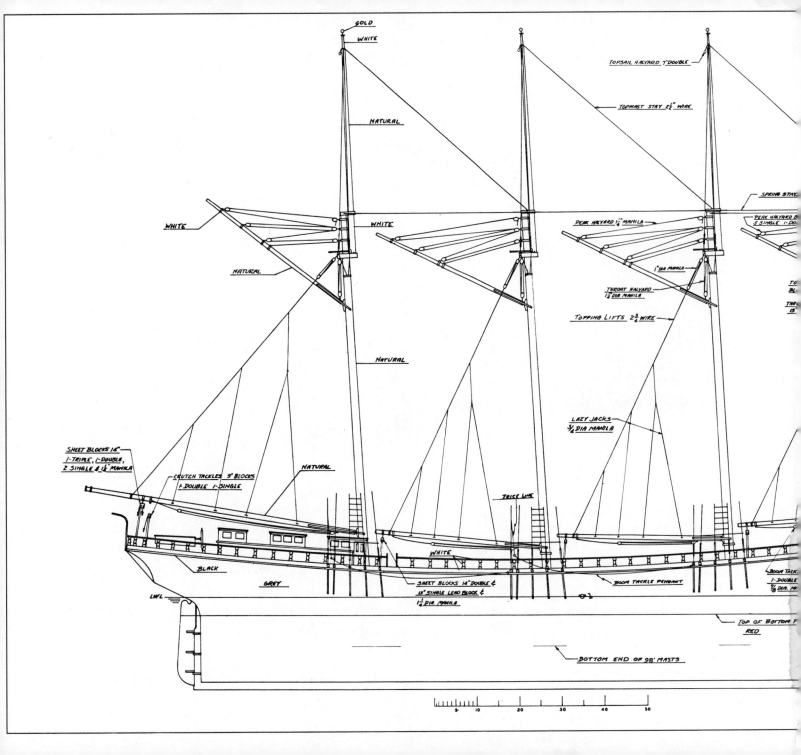

GOLD

WHITE

NATURAL

WHITE

TOPSAIL HALYARD T'DOUBLE

TOPMAST STAY 2⅛" WIRE

SPRING STAY

PEAK HALYARD 1¾" MANILA

PEAK HALYARD
3 SINGLE 1-DO

WHITE

NATURAL

WHITE

1" DIA MANILA

THROAT HALYARD
1¾ DIA MANILA

TO
3

THR
13

NATURAL

TOPPING LIFTS 2¾ WIRE

LAZY JACKS
¾ DIA MANILA

NATURAL

SHEET BLOCKS 18"
1-TRIPLE, 1-DOUBLE,
2 SINGLE & 1¼ MANILA

CRUTCH TACKLES 9" BLOCKS
1-DOUBLE 1-SINGLE

NATURAL

TRICE LINE

BOOM TACK
1-DOUBLE
⅞ DIA. MA

WHITE

BLACK

GREY

SHEET BLOCKS 14" DOUBLE &
12" SINGLE LEAD BLOCK &
1¼ DIA MANILA

BOOM TACKLE PENDANT

TOP OF BOTTOM P
RED

LWL

BOTTOM END OF 98' MASTS

|....|....|....|....|....|....|....|....|....|....|
       5   10   20   30   40   50

On the day of her launch in September 1919 the HERBERT L. RAWDING showed off her freshly painted bow and her headgear. Note the simple scrollwork and billethead; very few large schooners were adorned with figureheads. In the background, the frames of the MAURICE R. THURLOW illustrate the way the RAWDING was framed. There is still rigging work to be done aboard the RAWDING. The staysail and jib sheets have not yet been rove, nor have the tail ropes. Note the changes evident when comparing this view with the port bow view taken at Perth Amboy twenty-two years later. (Courtesy Andrew J. Nesdall)

Taken during re-rigging at Perth Amboy in 1941, this view shows details of the RAWDING's port bow. The vertical steel strapping around the hawsepipe protected the bow planking from damage if the patent anchor was hove in when a sea was running. Below the strapping, the four short planks of the timber port, or bow port, show clearly. These would be removed to take in pilings or timbers too long to fit through the deck hatches. Inside, two heavy vertical timbers rested on the frames of the port. The bow-port planks were bolted securely to these timbers, then the seams were caulked, cemented, and painted over. A good mate supervised this process with care, for these ports were subjected to tremendous pressure as the bow surged through the seas. Note the two scuppers for the forepeak and crew's head aft of the hawsehole. The ferry in the background ran from Perth Amboy to Tottenville, Staten Island. (Courtesy G.I. Johnson)

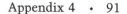

The intricate tracery of rigging on the foremast looks too delicate to withstand the terrible forces of several thousand tons of ship and cargo, and the wrenching strain of the 140-foot masts when huge seas tossed the vessel or hurricane winds shrieked and tore at anything loose or weakened. Yet, the RAWDING survived many such storms. Note that she had wooden battens rather than ratlines on her shrouds. Like other big schooners, the RAWDING had a double spring stay between fore and mainmast. The main gaff topsail is furled, but the fore topsail is not yet bent on, nor has all the rigging been set up. (Courtesy G.I. Johnson)

With the new foremast installed, the shipyard riggers have left a clutter of gear, including a twist in the throat halyard (visible against the mast), for the crew to straighten out. The open hatch on the port side of the forecastle head gave access to the forepeak, which contained the crew's head to port and a stowage area for some of the bosun's equipment (anything that would not tempt the crew to pilfer). Atop the forward house, the large stack forward was for the donkey engine. The smaller stack aft was for the galley range. When under way, the weather end of each stack was capped so the smoke would draw away to leeward (the starboard end of the forward stack is capped in this photo). When tacking ship, the crew was supposed to shift covers, and was often reminded of that fact by an irate cook or engineer whose place of business was suddenly filled with smoke pouring back the wrong way. (Courtesy G.I. Johnson)

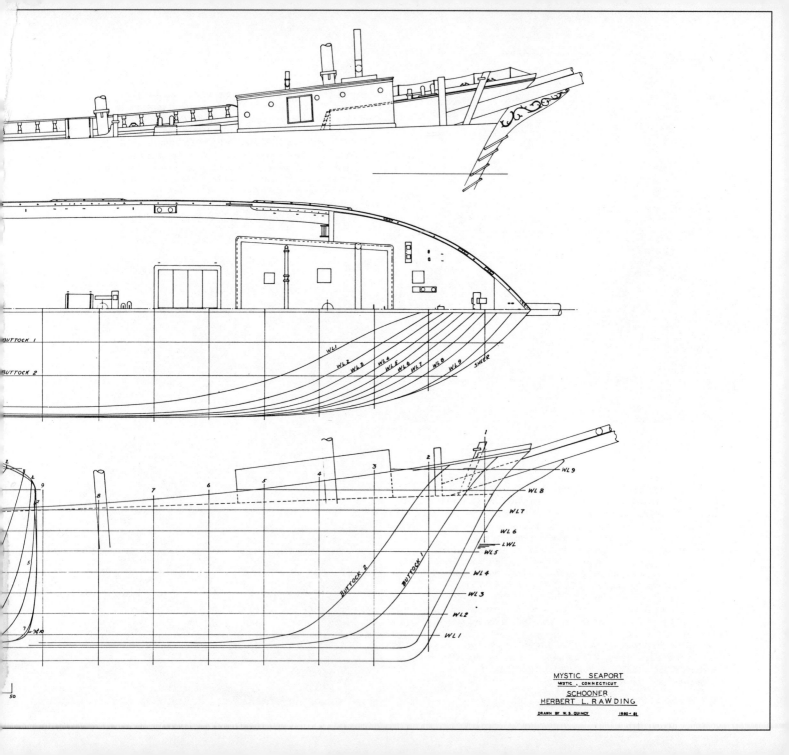

BUTTOCK 1

BUTTOCK 2

WL1
WL2
WL3
WL4
WL5
WL6
WL7
WL8
WL9
SHEER

BUTTOCK 2
BUTTOCK 1

WL 9
WL 8
WL 7
WL 6
LWL
WL 5
WL 4
WL 3
WL 2
WL 1

50

MYSTIC SEAPORT
MYSTIC , CONNECTICUT
SCHOONER
HERBERT L. RAWDING
DRAWN BY W.S. QUINCY   1980 - 81

On the port side of the forward house the crew's quarters were forward, and the galley aft. The shaft for the port winch head passed right through the galley. Just above the winch head, a bell-pull allowed the winch tender to signal for power. One bell called for power, two meant reverse, and one bell also meant stop. An experienced "chief" could often sense the needs of the winch tenders and speed up or slow the procedure if he felt undue strain on the gear. The big U-bolt on the corner of the house was used to hang a snatch block for special leads to the winch head.
(Courtesy G.I. Johnson)

The forward bits were used to secure downhauls for all the headsails, as well as the jib sheet and tail ropes. The two turnbuckles with a batten between them are for the foremast jumper stays. The RAWDING had a rather clumsy, unseamanlike arrangement at the foot of the forestay, just aft of the jumper stays. Rather than the usual tripod and gooseneck for the staysail club, she had a T-shaped metal fitting to which the club was lashed. The forestay was secured to the fitting with deadeyes, and the fitting was attached to the deck with two lengths of chain shackled to eyebolts.
(Courtesy G.I. Johnson)

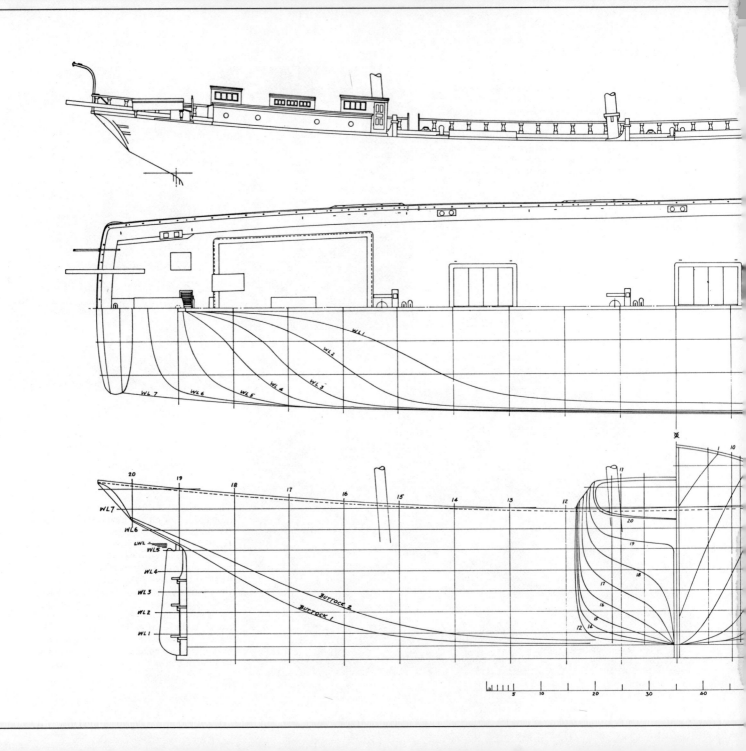

WL1

WL2

WL3

WL4

WL5

WL6

WL7

20   19   18   17   16   15   14   13   12

WL7
WL6
LWL
WL5
WL4
WL3
WL2
WL1

BUTTOCK 2
BUTTOCK 1

1   10

11

20

19

18

17

16

15   14

12   13

5   10   20   30   40

The outer end of the fore gaff shows the arrangement of the cheek block through which the topsail sheet was rove. Presumably the bar across the end of the wythe could have been used to secure a vang. Just forward of the cheek block is a band to reinforce the visible fracture in the gaff. Forward of that is the peak cringle band, with tangs on the bottom side. Although that peak halyard block should have been removed and repaired, it did not cause any trouble during my time in the vessel. (Courtesy G.I. Johnson)

This photo of the main sheet shows the sheet lead and the various fittings on the end of the boom. The sheet is rove through two double blocks, then through a tail block, and made fast on the bitt. The line with the large eye splice, which leads from the boom to the far side of the bitt, is a boom stop. The band at the end of the boom is the wythe, which keeps the end of the boom from splitting as the sun dries it out; the hook on the end is used for hauling the reef earing out when reefing. The next band has tangs through which the clew is bolted. There is no outhaul to adjust the foot in yacht style. Above that can be seen the peak downhaul on the gaff — a single line run around the end of the gaff through an eye splice, then forward and down along the boom. Forward of the sheet band is the angled band to which the topping lift is shackled, and forward of that is the band for the boom tackle. On the forward side of the mizzen mast, note the jaw ropes spliced across the open ends of the gaff and boom jaws to keep them from jumping clear of the mast. (Courtesy G.I. Johnson)

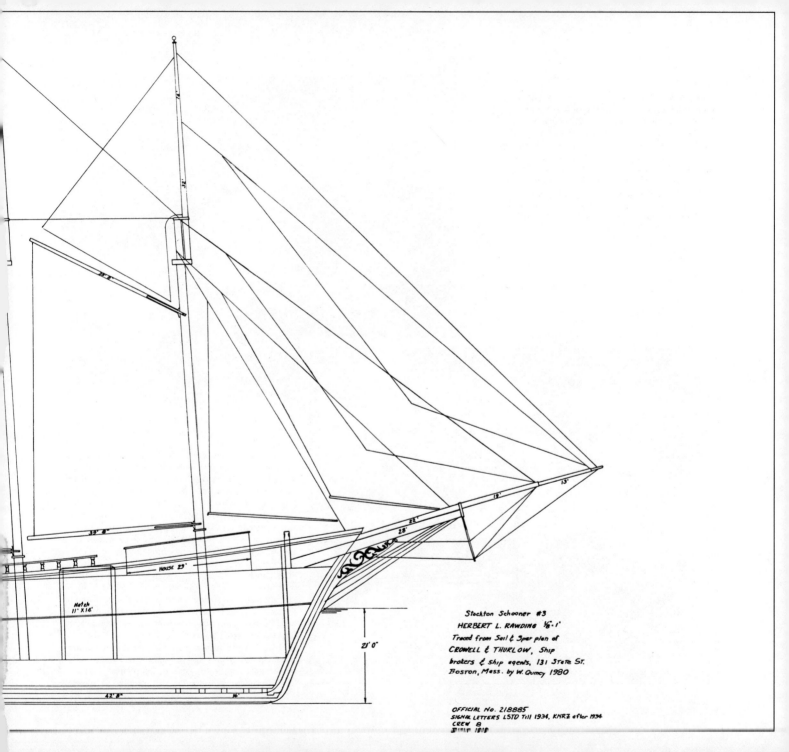

Stockton Schooner #3
HERBERT L. RAWDING ⅛=1'
Traced from Sail & Spar plan of
CROWELL & THURLOW, Ship
brokers & ship agents, 131 State St.
Boston, Mass. by W. Quincy 1980

OFFICIAL No. 218885
SIGNAL LETTERS LSTD Till 1934, KNRZ after 1934.
CREW 8

The forward companionway to the after house was called the "coach house." Having a door on either side allowed access on either tack in bad weather, and the window gave the mate, bosun, or cook a chance to gauge conditions on deck before venturing out, especially if the decks were awash in heavy weather. The iron bollards on the waterways in the foreground were used to secure spring lines in port. The bosun's room, located inside the first porthole, had a cramped little bunk right under the deck. The canvas hose from the scupper on top of the house was used to fill a water barrel when it rained. (Courtesy G.I. Johnson)

The after companionway was sacred to the master and invited guests. The rods attached to it helped strengthen the structure and also kept the boom tackle and other loose lines, such as lazy jacks, from snagging the structure when tacking or jibing. The binnacle box next to the life preserver contained the steering compass and a light to illuminate it at night. On the side not used for the light might be kept a cleaning rag, perhaps a white flare for warning off an approaching steamship, or a pair of binoculars. The small cask atop the house was a water breaker to be taken in the boat in the event of disaster. The bell (between the companionway and the after supporting rod) was used by the helmsman. When he heard the cabin clock chime he would step from the wheel and repeat the number of chimes. At night the lookout would answer, check the sidelights, and, if all was well, call to the mate, "lights are bright, sir!" The mate might reply with a grumpy "Alright!"
(Courtesy G.I. Johnson)

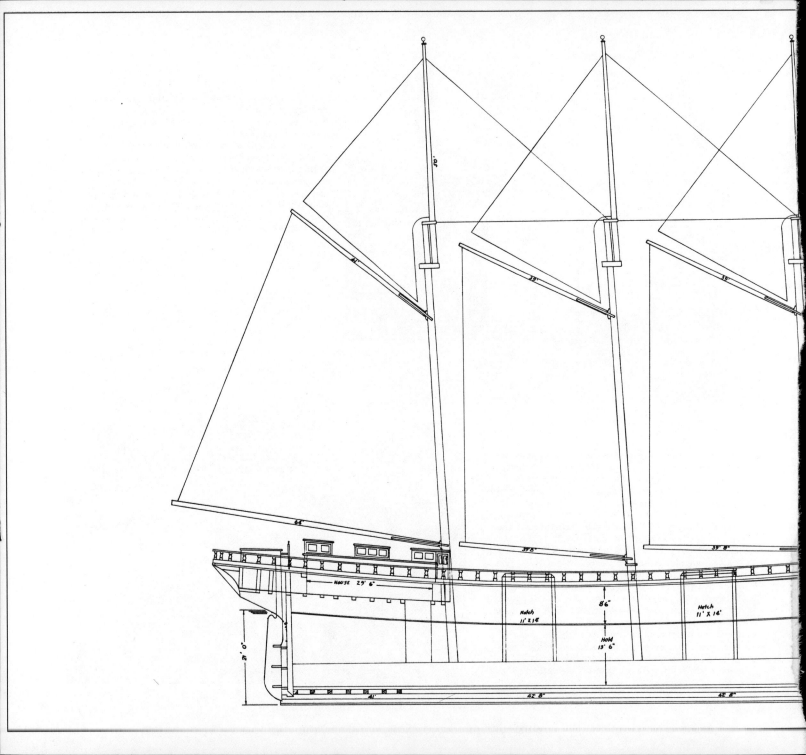

NOTES

1 W.J. Lewis Parker, *The Great Coal Schooners of New England, 1870-1909* (Mystic: Marine Historical Association, 1948), pp. 86-101.

2 John Lyman, "History of Crowell and Thurlow, Boston: Largest Schooner Fleet in the World," *Sea Breezes* 22 (November 1937): 174-75.

3 *Ibid.*

4 *Ibid.*

5 See the *Rawding Family Record*. Captain Herbert L. Rawding was born at Clementsport, Nova Scotia, in 1868. The small village of Clementsport produced fourteen Rawding master mariners between 1771 and 1964. An undated Boston newspaper article noted that five Rawding brothers commanded Crowell & Thurlow vessels at one time: Herbert L. Rawding, S.S. *Peter H. Crowell*; James E. Rawding, bark *Rekia*; John B. Rawding, schooner *Ellen Little*; Robert C. Rawding, schooner *Stanley M. Seaman*; and Llewellyn S. Rawding, coasting barge *Badger*.

6 Between 1918 and 1921 the Stockton yard built six four-masted schooners: 1918—*Helen Swanzey* (aux.), 746 tons gross, *Gladys M. Taylor*, 967 tons gross; 1919—*A Ernest Mills*, 946 tons gross, *Herbert L. Rawding*, 1206 tons gross; 1920—*Maurice R. Thurlow*, 1209 tons gross; 1921—*Alcaeus Hooper*, 1305 tons gross.

The *Helen Swanzey* was built for R.G. Morris of New York, and was soon sold to British interests. The remaining five were all for the Atlantic Coast Company. The *Gladys M.*

Taylor was lost by stranding in Penobscot Bay in 1929. The *A. Ernest Mills* was sunk in a collision with the U.S.S. *Childs* off Currituck, North Carolina, in 1929 while loaded with salt. When the salt melted, the hull rose to the surface and was destroyed by the Coast Guard as a menace to navigation. The *Maurice R. Thurlow* went about her business until she stranded on Diamond Shoal, off Cape Hatteras, in 1927. The *Alcaeus Hooper* foundered about 300 miles east of Cape Henry in 1924.

7 Captain Holden does not appear in the documentation; rather, Captain John J. Irons is listed. See Appendix 2.

8 Although the *New York Maritime Register* says she was laid up at the Meridian Street Bridge between Chelsea and Boston, she lay at T Wharf, Boston, for several months, and was photographed and sketched there. See Z. William Hauk, *T Wharf* (Boston: Alden-Hauk, 1952), p. 75.

9 In an article on the chemical uses of blackstrap molasses, the *Rawding* was illustrated, in a photograph from 1930, as the last sailing vessel to deliver a cargo of blackstrap molasses, as tankers were now delivering such cargo in bulk. This was probably true of blackstrap, but edible molasses continued to be shipped in wooden puncheons and hogsheads; some may yet be shipped in this manner. See *Monsanto Magazine*, April 1946.

10 William H. Swan & Sons had sold supplies to sailing vessels for many years and had interests in many of them. When times became hard for schooner captains, he is known to have given financial aid to many of them and was on the

board of governors of Sailors' Snug Harbor on Staten Island, where many an impoverished old seaman lived out his declining years.

11 George Torrey, the oldest brother, became a master at an early age and seems to have broken in his younger brothers as they became old enough to take to the sea. George and Delmont were lost at sea, while Winsor and Ernest died ashore.

Mrs. Winsor Torrey listed many of the schooners in which her husband sailed. As mate he sailed in the three-masters *Elm City* and *Emily L. White*; the four-masters *Massasoit, Bertha L. Downs,* and *Rachel W. Stevens*; and the five-masters *Magnus Manson* and *Edna Hoyt*. As master he commanded the three-masters *Helen Benedict, Abbie C. Stubbs, Helen Montague, Edward C. Blake, Frank Brainerd, Thomas H. Lawrence,* and *Albert H. Willis*; the four-masters *Addison E. Bullard, Charles Whittemore, David Cohen* (aux), *Charles H. MacDowell, Mary G. Maynard, Freeman, Hesper, Luther Little, Mohawk, Alvena,* and *Herbert L. Rawding*. During World War II he was master of a small steamship, the *Col. Lewis F. Garrad*, which served the forts about Boston Harbor. *Maine Coast Fisherman*, 1959.

12 Captain Torrey's journal is owned by his daughter.

13 The story of this voyage appeared in somewhat different form in *Ships and the Sea* magazine as "South in the *Herbert L. Rawding*," March 1952, and "Homeward Passage," September 1952.

14 From the National Archives in Washington, D.C., I received copies of letters between Intercontinental Steamship, John Mann, chief of the Warrants Section of the War Shipping Administration, and a host of would-be agents and shippers who wished to send cargo to South Africa in the *Herbert L. Rawding* and *Constellation*, as well as the four-masters *Theoline* and *Lewis K. Thurlow*. These documents reveal the questionable practices of Intercontinental Steamship.

15 Through the courtesy of the Newfoundland Museum at St. John's I have been able to reconstruct the final chapter of the *Rawding's* career from the people who bought her, the man who commanded her, and another who took charge of the engines that seem to have caused her demise.

Freeman Wareham of Alberto Wareham, Ltd., at Arnold's Cove, Newfoundland, had purchased the *Rawding* in 1945. In 1980 he wrote:

I am running a fairly large supermarket at Arnold's Cove with a small staff and do not have much spare time, I can assure you. You will see my father started this business out on an island about ten miles from Arnold's Cove. We done a large fishery business with banking schooners and large three-masted vessels to carry the fish to market. We bought three or five of these vessels in Denmark and Sweden.

In 1920 my father bought another premises about twenty miles away from Spencers Cove and I took charge of the business at Spencer Cove in May 1920. We moved here to Arnold's Cove in 1964. Our sales were a million-and-a-half dollars in 1979 . . . .

The *Rawding's* last master, Alex Rodway, lives in Toronto, and in several letters and on tape he outlined his life and the vessels he had commanded.

I also corresponded with the late Captain Victor Butler, who supervised installation of the *Rawding's* engines in 1946.

16 The *Robert W. Hart* was bound from Philadelphia to Naples, and dropped her passengers off at Gibraltar. Here the crew was supplied with clothing at the British facilities. Most of the crew was immediately shipped to England and home, but Captain Rodway remained a couple of weeks while a letter of protest was filed and an insurance investigation completed.

According to Captain Rodway, the crew consisted of mate Thomas Ashbourne, second mate George Upshall, donkeyman Calvin Gilbert, chief engineer George Pomeroy, second engineer Freeman Gilbert, cook Wallace Dicks, steward Ted Porter, and deckhands William Follett, John Flynn, Lewis Paul, and Isaac Peach. Their monthly pay in 1947 was about three times what it would have been five years earlier, and probably seemed good wages. The captain received $300, the mate $200, and the deckhands $100.

Captain Rodway returned to Newfoundland and for a couple of years ran a small steamer, the *Ilex*, owned by Alberto Wareham, Ltd., to run lobsters to the United States. About the end of 1948 he decided to leave the sea and proceeded to Toronto. Never having sought work ashore, he had no idea how to go about it, but scouted around, met a friend, and obtained work as a maintenance man in a large office building for the winter. Finally he landed a job on a ferry and sent for his family. He later went to Niagara Falls and commanded one of the *Maid of the Mist* excursion boats there. After eight years he retired, and returned to Toronto. He commented to me: "I have come to the time of life when one is shoulderd off the stage of former activities, but still have a comfortable stall to look through as spectator. Life has been good to us."